M E D
I C I
N A L
C H E F

The
# MEDICINAL
# CHEF

# THE POWER
# OF THREE

### The 3 nutritional secrets to a longer, healthier life in 80 simple recipes

## DALE PINNOCK

Photography by Martin Poole

QUADRILLE

## THE POWER OF THREE

In my line of work, there is one burning question that seems to come up time and time again. The one thing that everyone wants to know in the midst of this media barrage of conflict and contradiction around the subject of nutrition is: 'what IS the right diet?' The conflicting information and sensationalist headlines reported on the back of small studies and theories have created a consumer that is both hungry for health information, yet ultimately confused. Is it raw food, cooked food, gluten-free, dairy-free, high-fat, low-fat, meat, meat-free, paleo, macrobiotic, five-a-day, seven-a-day? There is a never-ending stream of information, all equally compelling. I would love to come up with a single, one-sentence answer that could finally put this to bed. Sadly, that isn't possible.

Nutrition is an ever-expanding and evolving science, a science that has seen a few major catastrophes over the years, such as the low-fat scandal I will talk about later. However, there are certainly some very strong patterns of evidence emerging about the role food plays in many of the modern-day diseases that are becoming epidemic in our society. With this in mind, I believe that there are three factors we should be aware of when thinking about the type of 'diet' to follow. When we employ these, we won't suddenly have all the answers, but we will be hedging our bets and coming as close to the ideal diet as we possibly can get. I truly believe that by addressing these three areas, we will be reducing our risk of the dietary-induced diseases that are plaguing us, and I will explain to you how and why.

So, what am I talking about? The Power of Three: blood sugar balance, fatty acid balance, and nutrient density.

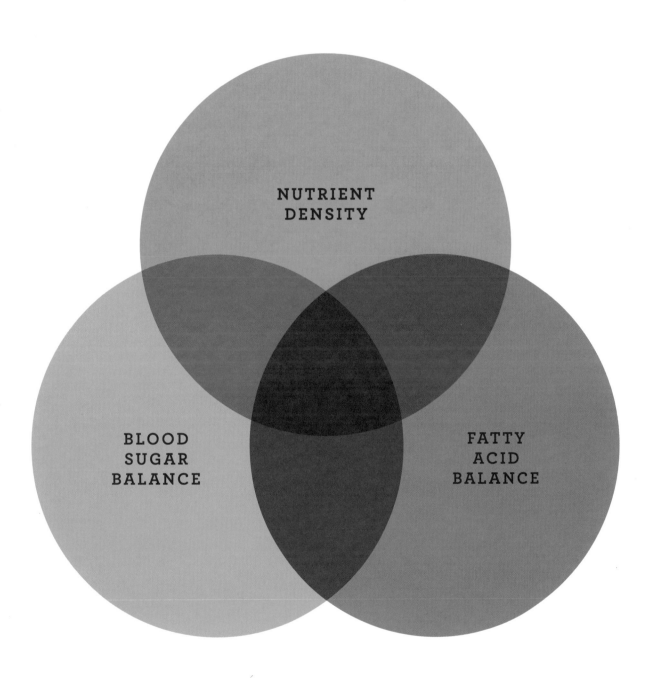

NUTRIENT
DENSITY

BLOOD
SUGAR
BALANCE

FATTY
ACID
BALANCE

# BLOOD SUGAR BALANCE

What is blood sugar? As you might expect, it is the glucose in circulation in our blood, and our cells use it to create a substance called ATP (adenosine triphosphate), which in turn is the fuel source that our cells need to carry out their multitude of daily functions. The level of glucose needs to stay within a very narrow range at all times. You might think, as it is such an important fuel source, that the more you have the better. But, no; things are never that simple as far as our bodies are concerned. If our blood sugar levels get too high or too low, then we are in trouble. When it is allowed to get too low, be it through not eating enough, not eating the right foods, or not eating for long periods of time, then we start to experience feelings of weakness and lack of concentration. Our energy dips and our mental performance is noticeably impaired. Most of all, we get hungry! If this continues, we can become paranoid and aggressive, and eventually we can even pass out. If it gets severe, then we run the risk of inducing a coma or even death. In answer to this, our body has a very powerful mechanism to prevent this from happening.

Our body stores glucose by converting it into glycogen and storing it in the liver and in muscle tissue. When our blood sugar levels begin to fall, we start to utilise these reserves; the pancreas releases a hormone called glucagon which takes glycogen out of storage and converts it back into glucose for use. This series of events also causes a release in the hormones that stimulate hunger and appetite. Low blood sugar has the potential to be very dangerous, but it is difficult to get to this state, as the urge to eat is too strong. Therefore the likelihood of low blood sugar being an issue for many people is low.

The real worry is when our blood sugar gets too high for too long; this is causing untold damage to our bodies today and is due to the way in which our diets have changed over the last 40-plus years. Blood sugar rises when simple sugars are liberated from the food we eat and then enter our circulation. At that point, cells in the pancreas, called beta cells, begin to secrete the hormone insulin. What insulin does initially is let our cells know that there is sugar available for use. It binds to specialised insulin receptors on cells, wakes them up and activates mechanisms on the outer surface of our cells, called glucose transporters. These shuttle glucose inside the cell where it can be converted into ATP, the cells' primary energy source (see above). Normally, we should have the perfect balance between glucose coming in from dietary sources, glucose being stored as glycogen, and insulin stimulating an increased glucose uptake by our cells. However, this isn't always the case, and in modern times the dreadful food so many people are eating is causing this system to break down. Our blood sugar levels should be drip-fed consistently. However, nowadays we are consuming diets that aggressively carpet-bomb our blood sugar! The negative consequences of this in the longer term are disastrous. It is one of the keys to the public-health crisis we are facing right now.

# HOW POOR BLOOD SUGAR CONTROL IS LINKED TO DISEASE

*Type-2 diabetes and insulin resistance*

The first and most obvious way that our modern diet is ruining our health via its impact upon blood sugar is through diabetes and the lesser-known insulin resistance – sometimes called 'prediabetes'. These conditions were not particularly prevalent even 20 years ago. They affected a few people, but most diabetics had Type 1, which you are born with or develop in early life. Type-2 diabetes has now become a serious issue, and one that could very soon reach proportions that could be described as epidemic. Insulin resistance is the first stage of the disease.

When we eat, food is digested and broken down into its constituent parts: the macronutrients (proteins, fats, carbohydrates) and micronutrients (vitamins, minerals, trace elements etc.), which enter the bloodstream following absorption and are shipped around to different places to do different jobs. When sugars from our diet enter the bloodstream, our body releases insulin in response. As we have seen, the insulin will then bind to its receptor and cause glucose transporters to spring into action, causing the cells to take in glucose. When this is going on at normal levels, everything works beautifully. However, when we eat foods that are very high in simple sugars, or that release their sugars rapidly, insulin levels rocket. If this happens now and again, it poses no threat to our health whatsoever.

So: you eat a chocolate bar, your blood sugar shoots up super-high super-fast, there is a larger insulin surge, the cells suck up the sugar – and job done. The problem arises when our entire diet consists of processed foods, refined carbohydrates and simple sugars, and this response happens all of the time. Blood sugar levels constantly soar and larger than usual levels of insulin are secreted. After a while, the cells start to get a little suspicious of insulin's behaviour and disbelieve what it is telling them; they think it has gone a bit crazy. So they start to ignore a lot of what it is saying. In short, they become resistant to the message that insulin is trying to deliver. Receptors don't pay attention to insulin, the body starts to become insulin resistant and the consequence is that blood sugar levels begin to rise and stay high for longer. The body responds by secreting more insulin, which works for a while. Then the cells' suspicions deepen and the whole situation deteriorates. This is when we are in a state of prediabetes.

Next comes the transition from prediabetes to full-blown Type-2 diabetes. When our cells become insulin resistant and blood sugar levels stay high, numerous problems can develop, one of which is something called glucotoxicity. This is the stage at which the level of sugar present can cause damage to tissues. It is believed that glucotoxicity may cause the beta cells to start to malfunction by damaging their internal components and causing increased oxidative stress – and then diabetes strikes. At this point, a doctor would prescribe daily insulin injections.

*Cardiovascular disease*
When we think about dietary risk factors for cardiovascular disease, the ones that first spring to mind are fat and fast food. These certainly have the potential to be damaging (although fat isn't the enemy we once thought it was), but one area that is completely overlooked is blood sugar balance. On the surface, there may not seem to be an obvious link between blood sugar and heart health, but when we unpack it a little, we will soon understand why it is so important.

As we have seen, blood sugar needs to stay within a very narrow, specific range. If it gets too low, we release stored glucose in the form of glycogen. If it gets too high, we secrete insulin that tells cells to open their doors and take in glucose to use for energy. Here is where things can go awry. Our cells are not ever-expansive glucose larders; there is a limit to how much glucose they can take in at any one time. If we are following the type of diet that causes blood sugar to stay consistently high, then sooner or later our cells will get dangerously full, albeit temporarily. However, there is a back-up plan for its removal: excess sugar can be converted into fat. Or rather, it is converted into a substance called triacylglycerol, otherwise known as triglycerides, the fats that are transported around our body in the bloodstream. You may be familiar with this term if you have had blood tests during a check up with your doctor.

Triglycerides are a risk factor for cardiovascular disease because they are very susceptible to oxidative damage. When they become oxidised, they can cause localised inflammation and damage within our blood vessel walls, which is the trigger for the series of events that ultimately lead to heart disease. Inflammation is the trigger for atherosclerosis, the fatty calcified plaques that form in the walls of the vessels. I will go into a bit more detail about this later on when I talk about fatty acids (see page 21). Triglycerides travel around the body on a specialised carrier called VLDL (very low density lipoprotein), during which process VLDL is converted into LDL (you guessed it – low density lipoprotein). This is the substance that has been nicknamed 'bad cholesterol' and for which millions of people are under drug treatment to try to reduce. So much importance is placed upon a low-fat diet when it comes to heart health, but sadly many of the foods that we have been recommended can inadvertently make matters much worse.

*Obesity*

We are in the throes of an obesity epidemic; millions of us struggle with extra weight, and for many, the battle is fruitless. I feel incredibly strongly about the nonsense that is being touted today to myriad eager dieters. There are vast corporations that have built their business models on these outdated concepts. I'm not going to go into great detail about my feelings on the matter (that's for another book!) but I will say that the 'calories in, calories out – burn more than you eat' model is drivel. It is physiologically flawed and will never deliver permanent weight management. I have had so many requests to include calorie information in my recipes but: no way, never gonna happen!

One of the major things we need to become aware of is the macronutrient composition of our diets. Macronutrients are the biggies – proteins, fats and carbohydrates. The amount we consume and the impact these have on our metabolism are the key issues. Enter: blood sugar control. During the public health fiasco of the late 1950s, we were all encouraged to adopt a 'healthy low-fat diet' and replace fatty foods with starchy foods such as bread, pasta and potatoes. This is where the problem started. There is nothing wrong with these foods *per se*. The problem is the quantity we are eating and the form that these foods take. Whilst they can indeed be healthy, they have the capacity to deluge our blood with glucose rapidly and extensively. Eaten in small amounts, they are fine. But how's this for a typical scenario that most of us can relate to: breakfast is a bowl of cereal and a slice of toast, lunch is a sandwich, dinner may be meat, veg and potatoes, curry and rice, pasta, maybe even a slice of bread to clean the plate with. That sounds pretty average, right? Well, that is excessive and the impact that this eating has on blood sugar is unbelievable.

As we have seen above, once our cells have taken in as much glucose as they can in one sitting, the remainder is converted into triglycerides which attach to lipoproteins (VLDL) for transportation. But where are they transported to? Our adipose tissue, otherwise known as body fat! We have a double whammy effect here, because in addition to this effect, insulin, which rises when blood sugar does, has another massive metabolic role. That is to open the gates in our adipocytes (fat cells) to let triglycerides enter for storage. This is a normal response built deeply into our physiology and meant for our survival. When insulin drops down again, these triglycerides are able to come back out of adipocytes and go back into circulation where they can be used as an easily accessible energy source. However, as long as insulin is high, this remains a one-way flow of traffic. Triglycerides flow in to the adipocytes and stay there: we accumulate fat. What one factor keeps our insulin high and keeps us making triglycerides? Continually high blood sugar.

## HOW DO WE ADDRESS THIS VIA DIET?

The picture I've painted looks a little grim, I know, but there is a great deal that we can do about it! It really is in our hands. A few simple changes to our daily diet can prevent the series of events. Even if you have been eating badly for years and are starting to develop or have developed issues as a result, these changes will still offer benefits and are perfectly safe.

*Reduce your intake of refined carbohydrates*
Carbohydrates really do come in 'the good, the bad and the ugly'. When we digest carbohydrates, we liberate their sugars from the foods that we are eating. Some carbohydrates take a lot of digestive effort and therefore their sugars are liberated

slowly, gently and evenly, and released into the bloodstream in a more drip-fed fashion. Others are so refined and simple or contain so much sugar, that they take very little digestive effort to release them and they flood the bloodstream with glucose rapidly. Keep away from, or greatly reduce, white bread, white rice, white pasta, potatoes, granulated sugar, sweets etc. These are the foods that will assault your bloodstream with a tidal wave of glucose and cause all of the above. I think it's a good idea to reduce the amount of starchy foods that we eat in general, but the ones you do eat should be in their wholewheat/wholegrain forms, e.g. brown rice, multigrain bread etc. These have more fibre in them, which takes more digestive effort to liberate the sugars, meaning they are absorbed slower and more evenly.

*Properly combine your meals*
The way in which our meals are composed will have a massive impact on how quickly they are digested, and how quickly the sugars from the meal are released into the bloodstream. The simple rule here is to always combine proteins and carbohydrates at each meal. This could be along the lines of poached eggs on toast, chicken and chickpea salad, baked salmon with sweet potato mash and green vegetables. You get the picture!

By consuming meals that are composed in this way, the protein holds the meal in the stomach longer, only releasing a fraction of it at a time into the small intestine where carbohydrate digestion and absorption take place. You have multiple benefits. Eating in such a way results in a slow and steady release of blood sugar, but it also keeps you fuller for longer, meaning you eat less. And finally, these combinations mean that you get a greater variety of foods in your diet throughout the day.

FATTY
ACID
BALANCE

Fat is one of the most feared aspects of our diet, and is still believed by many to be the nutritional demon, certain to catapult you to an early grave. This fear and fanaticism all stemmed from a fiasco in the 1950s. This transformed the developed world's diet forever, massively to our detriment.

In the last four to five decades, the patterns of fat intake in the Western diet have changed drastically. This is largely due to the work of a man called Ancel Keys. Keys was an American physiologist heavily involved in nutrition. He was the developer of the K-ration employed by the US military in the field. Keys came up with a hypothesis that the cause of cardiovascular disease was the intake of saturated fat, and that a country's intake directly correlated with the incidence of heart disease. He was a very ambitious chap and set out to prove this hypothesis with vigour. He designed a study of 22 countries in which he examined their diets and the correlation between saturated fat intake and cardiovascular disease. However, when the study was published, the data from only seven of the 22 countries was used, and the results looked very impressive indeed.

In fact, the data produced a beautiful positive curve, and essentially proved Keys's hypothesis that saturated fat intake was indeed associated with cardiovascular disease. But hang on a minute! From 22 countries to seven. What's going on here? As it turns out, the seven countries selected were the seven that actually supported his theory. Had he used all 22 countries, the evidence would have done nothing to link saturated fat and cardiovascular disease. What was published was in effect a fraudulent and engineered piece of reporting. The selective inclusion and exclusion of data proved something that didn't actually exist.

On publication, Ancel Keys became a hero. After a few months, he appeared on the cover of *Time* magazine, and in no time at all the American government was developing a public health campaign. It encouraged the population to ditch saturated fat, to make use of supposed 'heart healthy' oils like sunflower oil, margarine etc., and to move towards a diet high in starchy foods (see page 11 for the damage that did). The same public health message made it to the UK and then began to dominate the Western world. If we look at data from institutions such as the World Health Organization we can see that as these changes in our diets were implemented, and we moved towards more starchy foods and polyunsaturated oils, the incidence of diseases like heart disease, Type-2 diabetes and cancer began to soar and all of a sudden we were facing an obesity epidemic.

So, why did this happen? These fats are healthy, right? No! The problem with these vegetable oils is that they are composed predominantly of omega-6 fatty acids. These are essential components of our diet and they are vital for our body – but only in very small doses. In the UK, on average, we consume in the region of 23 times more than we need per DAY!

Let me backtrack a moment and break down why this is such a problem. Essential fatty acids are fat-derived compounds that our bodies require, amongst other roles, to provide the building blocks for a group of communication compounds called prostaglandins. Prostaglandins regulate certain responses in the body, such as the inflammatory response for example.

There are three distinct types of prostaglandin, called Series 1, Series 2, and Series 3. Series 1 is mildly anti-inflammatory. Series 2 is a very aggressive and powerful stimulator of inflammation, and an enhancer of pain. Series 3, on the other hand, is a potent inhibitor and reducer of inflammation and pain. Now, different dietary fatty acids are used to manufacture different prostaglandins. Omega-6 fatty acids (which we are unknowingly gorging on via the 'healthy' fats we're encouraged to consume) are the building blocks for the Series 2 prostaglandins. So our current omega-6-loaded diet is setting off and and accelerating inflammation. As a result, many of us are in a state of subclinical (i.e. without obvious symptoms like swelling), chronic (i.e. persisting for years) inflammation within tissues. This phenomenon has been linked to many of the biggest killers in the health of the Western world.

## HOW FATTY ACIDS ARE LINKED TO DISEASE

*Heart disease*
Heart disease is the biggest killer in the developed world. Fact. There are many risk factors, of varying degrees, that are associated with cardiovascular disease. One fact is clear,

though, and that is that cardiovascular disease is an inflammatory condition. The inside of our blood vessels is lined with a very thin layer called the endothelium. Inflammation can cause pockets of damage within this endothelium and the body responds immediately to repair it by laying down a delicate criss-cross lattice of fibres. Some of these fibres can protrude out into the vessel, a bit like a net. Materials that are in circulation in the blood, such as cholesterol, can get trapped in this net. Cholesterol can oxidise and cause further damage to the vessel walls. This damage continues until the immune system gets involved and a plaque is formed.

Low-grade chronic inflammation of the endothelium can also increase blood pressure. The endothelium is highly metabolically active. One of its main roles is to manufacture and release nitric oxide, which relaxes the muscular walls of the vessels, causing the vessel to reduce the pressure within it. Nitric oxide also protects the endothelium against damage. On-going mild inflammation can affect endothelial cells' ability to release nitric oxide.

So what causes this inflammation? Some of the more obvious agents include smoking, excessive drinking, and environmental pollutants. But the biggest factor in the modern world is the type of fats we are eating via vegetable oils and processed foods.

*Cancer*
Cancer is the second biggest killer in the Western world, and one that is increasing at an alarming rate. Today, one in three of us is likely to be in some way affected by the disease. That is a shocking statistic. It is important to understand that cancer is an outcome with a multitude of variables that may actually cause it. This is part of the reason why it has proved such a

difficult adversary to beat. Inflammation is but one of many links, but it is at least one that we can have some influence over. When tissues get inflamed for long periods of time, the DNA within them can eventually become damaged. DNA codes genes that determine how our cells function and what they do on a day-to-day basis. The damage to the DNA from chronic inflammation can affect genes that regulate the way in which cells divide and replicate. In short, cells can begin to divide uncontrollably, forming the early stages of a tumour. Inflammation is capable of a secondary attack, too, though. During the early stages of tumour growth, inflammation occurs in the area which can become involved in the generation of new blood vessels to the tumour; this triggers accelerated tumour growth to the point where a few rogue cells become cancer.

### Type-2 diabetes

I explained in the previous section regarding excessively high blood sugar and insulin how insulin resistance and Type-2 diabetes are initiated. However, there is another influence that can exacerbate it and that is of course inflammation. Chronic, low-grade inflammation has been shown to affect the functionality of insulin receptors. Insulin is already struggling to get cells to take notice during insulin resistance; inflammation makes matters worse, and the stage is soon set for the development of serious problems.

### Inflammatory disorders

It is to be expected that inflammatory conditions by nature should also be aggravated by this diet. Arthritis, eczema, psoriasis, inflammatory bowel disease – all of these can be activated by the wrong dietary choices.

## HOW DO WE ADDRESS THIS VIA DIET?

Effective results can be achieved with the smallest steps.
I have spoken about omega 6 and its propensity to stimulate
and aggravate inflammation. Now is the time to introduce
omega 6's happy, healthy, and all-round virtuous twin,
omega 3. The omega-3 fatty acids are the antidote to all this.
Whereas omega 6 is the metabolic building block for Series 2
prostaglandins, which switch on and worsen inflammation,
omega 3 is the one connected to the types of prostaglandin
that actually switch off and regulate inflammation. One
omega 3 fatty acid in particular, EPA, is the precursor to
the powerfully anti-inflammatory Series 3 prostaglandin.
So, the simple solution is to balance your intake of fatty acids.
Each day, you need to be consuming more omega 3 than
omega 6 so that your body is not pumping out too many
pro-inflammatory prostaglandins.

*Increase your intake of omega 3*
Aim to increase your intake of omega-3 fatty acids every
single day. The key foods here are oily fish, such as salmon,
mackerel, herrings, anchovies, sardines etc. There are those
who try to convince us that omega 3 found in seeds will deliver
the same benefits as those found in oily fish, but alas they won't.
I have had the great pleasure of working directly with the
world's leading authorities on fatty acids, from every continent.
There are a million and one facts that these academic and
clinical superpowers disagree on, but there is one thing that
every one of them is in agreement on – that marine-derived
omega-3 fatty acids deliver the most powerful and effective
protective benefits. Walnuts, flaxseeds, chia seeds etc. are
better than nothing, but they come in the form of the ALA
omega 3, which needs converting to EPA and DHA. We can
convert it into DHA extremely simply. But human beings

are very poor at converting ALA into EPA, succeeding with maybe eight to ten per cent if we are lucky. The only exception to this rule is pregnant women, who can ramp up conversion to many times this. So even if you eat gallons of the stuff, you will be getting microscopic traces of EPA, which delivers 90% of the benefits associated with omega 3. Some animals, such as fish, are exceptionally good at this conversion, which is why their tissues are packed with these vital fats.

If you are vegetarian (I understand; I was vegetarian for more than 20 years), be aware that there will, for now at least, be a nutritional gap in your diet. There is now technology to extract EPA from algae, and these supplements will soon be hitting the market. Once this happens, vegetarians will be easily catered for. Supplementation with highly concentrated EPA and DHA daily is also a good idea for everyone. Eating fish every day will get a little boring.

*Reduce your intake of omega 6*
The next step is to reduce your intake of omega-6 fatty acids, which is remarkably straightforward. The main focus will be the types of oils you use on a daily basis. If you are currently using vegetable oil, corn oil, sunflower oil, soy oil, and/or margarine, take a large bin bag, fill it with these oils and throw them in the dustbin, never to be seen again. These products are almost pure omega 6. Just the smallest spoonful will take you above and beyond your daily requirement, so tipping the balance is incredibly easy. When it comes to cooking oils, there are only two that I use: olive oil and coconut oil. Olive oil comprises largely a fatty acid called oleic acid which belongs to the omega-9 group. These fats have zero effect upon fatty acid balance whatsoever. Plus, oleic acid has benefits for heart health, too. Coconut oil is my go-to choice when I want to do any high-temperature work. Olive oil is

pretty heat-stable, but at high temperatures, like high-heat stir-frying or roasting, it can start to denature a little bit. Coconut oil is completely heat-stable, even at very high temperatures. Coconut oil also has the added benefit that it contains no polyunsaturated fatty acids (the types of fats that omega 3 and omega 6 belong to), so it has absolutely no impact upon fatty acid balance whatsoever. When it comes to replacing hideous margarines, I'd go for butter every time. Don't be scared of it; it is a million times better for you than margarines ever could be – just don't eat an entire pack a day! Your body knows what to do with these naturally occurring fats.

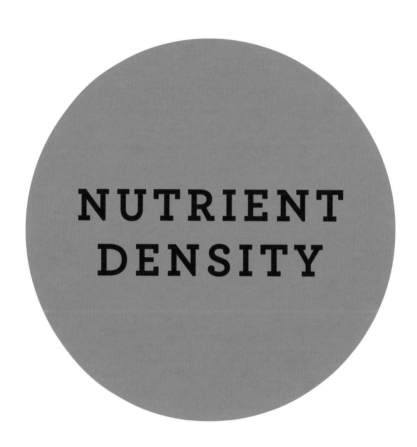

NUTRIENT DENSITY

One of the single most important cornerstones in devising a healthy diet is to go for maximal nutrient density. In an age of overly processed foods and convenience, the nutrient density of our diets is often very poor indeed. What exactly do I mean by 'nutrient density'? I mean foods that provide vast amounts of a broad spectrum of nutrients rather than just dead, empty calories; foods that deliver deep nourishment rather than just a bit of fuel.

Nutrients can be divided into three major classes: macronutrients, micronutrients and phytonutrients/phytochemicals. As I've mentioned already, macronutrients are the proteins, fats, and carbohydrates. Micronutrients are the vitamins, minerals and trace elements. Phytochemicals are the massive array of active components that aren't classified essential nutrients, but have untold benefits for the body.

Consider something like white pasta, for example. What we have here is a food that provides us with just one major macronutrient – carbohydrate – and not a lot else.

Throw in a jar of ready-made pasta sauce and you may have a little bit of vitamin C and iron, but still not a great deal for the amount of food and energy you are taking in. Now imagine a similar dish but made with wholewheat pasta and a simple sauce from red onions, garlic, fresh tomatoes, basil and pepper. It's neither expensive nor extravagant, but this time it has a much lower glycaemic impact and contains more vitamin C, magnesium, iron, and a host of phytochemicals such as carotenoids, flavonoids and ajoene. You have created a dish with a far superior level of nutrition.

## HOW DO WE ADDRESS THIS VIA DIET?

These are my ultra-simple strategies.

*Get fresh*

At each and every meal, look for opportunities to add fresh plant foods to your diet. This isn't as hard as it seems. Let's take breakfast, for example. If you start your day with something like porridge, simply top it with blueberries, raspberries, sliced banana – the list is endless. At lunch time, no matter what you normally have, there is always a chance to pack in more nutrient-dense ingredients. Say you have a sandwich; if you make it yourself, add fresh, raw baby spinach, maybe some fresh herbs or chopped spring onions. If you have something like a bowl of soup, then make yourself a good side salad to go with it. It is so very easy to find decent-quality prepared salads in most honest food outlets (don't even go near fast-food outlets), with many chains offering some fabulous selections. For your evening meal, if you are a meat, veg and potatoes kind of person, then great – potentially. Reduce the amount of potato you consume (that will have a much better

glycaemic impact too), and fill that space on your plate with fresh vegetables cooked in as many ways as you can imagine: simply sautéed with butter, curried, or stir-fried with garlic and Asian herbs. Whatever takes your fancy. Every meal presents you with an opportunity to get fresh plant foods into your diet. Each of these ingredients will be a powerhouse of vitamins, minerals, trace elements and phytochemicals.

### Eat a rainbow

This phrase is nothing new, but I must emphasise this extension of the Get Fresh information above. It is vital to incorporate different coloured fruits and vegetables into your diet – every day. Every colour represents a different spectrum of nutrients and phytochemicals, with lists of properties long enough to fill a tome. Orange foods are rich in carotenoids. Red and purple foods are rich in flavonoids, and so on. The more colour variation, the more nutritional variation.

### Choose better meats

The meat that you eat will have a huge impact on the overall nutrient density of your diet. The most commonly eaten meat in the UK is chicken. The amount of low-quality chicken that makes its way into the many ready meals, deli meats, restaurants etc. is mind-blowing. I won't touch on the ethical considerations surrounding the way in which these animals are reared; I will concentrate here on the poor nutrient density. Much of this low-grade, mass-produced chicken comes from animals that have been fed a hugely poor-quality, grain-based diet. The nutritional content of a meat is a direct reflection of the animal's diet, unsurprisingly. Where possible, opt for high-quality, free-range chicken. I know it can be expensive, so do it when you can. Other meats that I feel are much better options than low-quality chicken are high-quality red meats, game meats, organ meats, and of course oily fish. Organ meats, game meats and oily fish tend to have much more nutrition per gram. They are rich sources of selenium, zinc, iron, essential fatty acids, vitamin D and vitamin A.

## Keep it whole

In all situations, keep it whole. By that I mean always choose whole foods that are minimally processed and close to their natural form. So with foods like rice, go for the brown variety rather than the white which has had its B vitamin-rich outer husk removed. Breads: ditch white refined flour and choose wholemeal ones made with unrefined grains which are rich in B vitamins and various minerals. Use all of your vegetables, so use the stems of broccoli, keep the skins on your sweet potatoes; most of the minerals are present just beneath the skin. Make as many of your dishes from scratch from whole ingredients, rather than getting processed ready-made foods in. By opting for whole foods you will be getting more phytochemicals, minerals, fibre, vitamins – the works. You will be consuming wholesome, nutrient-rich foods rather than refined, dead mush.

## Cook to retain nutrients

The final part of the picture here is the way in which you prepare your food. Some cooking methods will completely annihilate nutrients, whereas others retain or improve the nutritional status of the ingredients. The ultimate in cooking methods to avoid is boiling! Many of the important nutrients such as the B vitamins, and vitamin C are water soluble; when we boil vegetables, all these important substances leach out and end up down the sink. The go-to cooking methods of choice for me are, sautéeing, stir-frying, steaming, baking and roasting.

## SO, WHEN CAN I START?!

The recipes in this book all bring together the three principles of blood sugar balance, fatty acid balance, and nutrient density. You may worry at first that you are having to learn a brand new way of eating. But before very long you will be doing this completely on autopilot; you will be able to make better choices every single day and build your entire life's diet on healthier foundations. Good luck, enjoy cooking and eating, and keep up the great work!

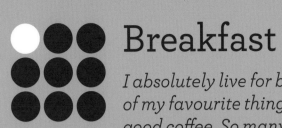

# Breakfast

*I absolutely live for breakfast. It is just one of my favourite things in life. Breakfast and good coffee. So many of us skip breakfast, and a very high proportion of us that do eat it, reach for processed cereals – which should be avoided like the plague! Breakfast represents the first opportunity of the day to get things right. These ideas should get you started on the right track.*

## Sweet potato rösti with garlic butter greens

This is a great, filling breakfast that takes very little time and effort. It's got masses of protein, carotenoids and fibre, and it's super slow burning – all kinds of good stuff!

**SERVES 1**

1 small sweet potato, scrubbed clean and grated
1 spring onion, chopped into matchsticks
1 tablespoon wholemeal flour (gluten-free flours are fine too)
1 large egg
olive oil, for frying
large handful greens (I like half and half kale and spinach)
2 teaspoons garlic butter

Place the grated sweet potato, spring onion and flour into a bowl and mix well. Crack in the egg and mix everything well again until it forms a batter-like mixture.

Heat a little olive oil in a frying pan until hot, then add the batter to the centre of the pan in a patty shape, making sure the ingredients are pressed down well and tightly compressed. Fry for 3–4 minutes each side or until golden and crispy, and held together.

Meanwhile, melt the garlic butter in a pan, add the greens and sauté until softened, then serve on top of the rösti.

## Homemade granola

Most shop-bought granola cereals are packed full of sugar and rubbish. This version still has a sweetness, but nowhere near the amount of added sugar and gunk that commercial ones have. It's perfect when you want a sweeter cereal-type breakfast that's still healthy.

**MAKES 200G, OR SERVES 3–4**
3 tablespoons runny honey
2 tablespoons light olive oil
1 teaspoon vanilla extract
2 teaspoons ground cinnamon
160g oats
2 tablespoons pumpkin seeds
2 tablespoons sunflower seeds
1 tablespoon flaxseeds
2 tablespoons chopped
  walnuts

Preheat the oven to 180°C/350°F/Gas mark 4 and line a baking tray with baking parchment.

Place the honey, oil, vanilla extract and cinnamon in a bowl with 2 tablespoons water. Whisk well to evenly combine.

Add the oats, seeds and walnuts and mix well to ensure that everything is completely coated. Spread the mixture evenly out on the lined baking tray.

Bake in the oven until dry, crispy and turning a lovely golden brown, 20–30 minutes. Keep tabs on it, and give it a stir a couple of times during baking.

## Spiced egg and sardines This may at first sound like a very weird combination indeed, but take a little leap of faith and give it a go.

**SERVES 1**

2 hard-boiled eggs
¼ teaspoon ground cumin
generous grind of
  black pepper
pinch of sea salt
1 tablespoon olive oil
2–3 fresh, prepared sardines
2–3 slices granary
  or rye bread
1 handful watercress

Preheat the grill to hot. Peel the hard-boiled eggs and transfer to a mixing bowl. Mash them roughly with a fork, then add the cumin, pepper, salt and olive oil, and mix well.

Grill the sardines for 3–4 minutes on each side, until the edges are beginning to turn a little golden, but before the skin crisps up.

Toast the bread. Spread the egg mixture on each slice of bread, scatter with the watercress, and then top with a sardine.

# Crab, avocado and coriander omelette with lime

This is a breakfast based on a wonderful early-morning treat I had at a hotel in Hong Kong that I have tweaked a little. This feels so indulgent, but is full of all the good stuff.

**SERVES 1**
2 large eggs
olive oil, for cooking
1 x 100g tin crab meat, drained
½ small, ripe avocado,
    peeled and thinly sliced
small bunch fresh coriander
juice of ½ lime
sea salt and black pepper

Crack the eggs into a bowl and whisk them vigorously for a few seconds.

Heat a little olive oil in a non-stick omelette pan and tip in the whisked eggs. Cook over a high heat until the egg is cooked on the underside, with just the smallest amount of uncooked egg on the top.

Place the crab meat and sliced avocado on one half of the omelette. Tear the coriander over, add salt and pepper to taste, then fold the uncovered half of omelette over the filling and cook for another 30 seconds. Transfer to a plate and squeeze over the lime juice before serving.

# King prawn and spring onion scramble

This is one of my favourite, quick weekend breakfasts. It takes minutes to make, yet tastes like something that is just a bit fancy.

**SERVES 1**

2 large eggs
2 teaspoons olive oil
1 large spring onion,
  sliced on the diagonal
75g cooked king prawns
1 teaspoon toasted
  sesame oil
sea salt

Crack the eggs into a bowl and whisk for a few seconds.

Heat the olive oil in a non-stick frying pan, add the spring onion and prawns and sauté until the onion begins to soften and the prawns are hot. Push them to one side of the pan to keep warm. Add the whisked eggs to the other side of the hot pan and stir continuously until they reach a scrambled egg texture.

Serve the spring onions and prawns over the scramble, drizzle over the sesame oil and season with salt to taste.

## Spinach and kipper baked eggs I am a massive fan of baked eggs. You really can throw all manner of combinations together quickly and easily, and it's a great way to use up leftovers!

**SERVES 1**
2 handfuls baby spinach
1 kipper fillet
2 large eggs
80g feta cheese
sea salt and black pepper

Preheat the oven to 200°C/400°F/Gas mark 6.

Gently steam-sauté the spinach in 1 tablespoon water in a pan for just long enough for it to wilt down nicely.

Cook the kipper by either boiling in the bag if you have a pre-packed one, according to the packet instructions, or under a hot grill for 10–12 minutes. Flake the flesh.

Mix together the spinach and flaked kipper in a small ovenproof dish and season with a little salt and pepper.

Make a couple of indentations and crack an egg into each. Crumble the feta over the top of the whole lot, then bake in the oven for 15 minutes, or until the eggs are fully cooked.

# Seedy coconut overnight oats

Overnight oats are basically the result of soaking oats…overnight. Who'd have thought it? Many purists believe that by not cooking the oats, more of the B vitamins remain intact. I'm not sure I buy this, personally, but I do love the texture that it gives.

**SERVES 1**

60g porridge oats
1 teaspoon pumpkin seeds
1 teaspoon sunflower seeds
1–2 drops vanilla extract
   (optional)
¼ teaspoon ground cinnamon
1 x 400ml tin coconut milk
1 teaspoon flaxseeds

Place the oats, pumpkin seeds, sunflower seeds, vanilla extract, if using, and the cinnamon in a bowl. Mix, then stir in about three-quarters of the coconut milk. Mix thoroughly and leave to soak overnight.

Just before serving, add the flaxseeds and the remaining coconut milk.

# Egg and bacon stuffed tomato

This unusual little breakfast is one of my favourite Saturday morning late breakfasts. Juicy and flavoursome!

**SERVES 1**

olive oil, for greasing
    and cooking
1 large egg
1 large beef tomato,
    top cut off like a lid,
    and insides scooped
    out to create a 'bowl'
1 rasher nitrate-free
    bacon, chopped
salt and black pepper

Preheat the oven to 200°C/400°F/Gas mark 6 and lightly oil a baking tray.

Whisk the egg in a bowl and heat a little oil in a non-stick pan. Tip in the egg and cook over a high heat, stirring for a minute or so, until it is just starting to scramble, but is still mostly liquid. Season with salt and pepper.

Place the hollowed-out tomato on the oiled baking tray and fill with the part-scrambled egg and the chopped bacon. Lay the tomato 'lid' on the tray, too

Cook in the oven for about 25 minutes, until the tomato skin has started to wrinkle and the egg filling is golden.

**Sticky bars** These are pretty painless to make and taste wonderful. They have a nice sticky-sweet vibe going on, but are extremely filling – the perfect option for when you need something portable that will keep you going when you are on the road or are going to be stuck in a meeting!

**MAKES ABOUT 16**
50g flaxseeds
50g chopped walnuts
15 pitted dates, chopped into small pieces
75g peanut butter
1 tablespoon desiccated coconut

Preheat the oven to 180°C/350°F/Gas mark 4.

Place half the flaxseeds and half the walnuts in a food processor and blitz into an almost powder-like texture. Mix this with the remaining flaxseeds and chopped walnuts and combine well. This will give the bars a variety of textures.

Cook the dates and 2 tablespoons water in a pan over a high heat for a few minutes, stirring continuously, until the dates begin to break down and form a paste. Add the peanut butter and mix well until combined.

Add the seed and nut mixture with the coconut, and combine well.

Press into a baking tin about 25 x 25cm, lined with baking parchment, and bake in the oven for about 20 minutes. Allow to cool completely before cutting into bars.

# On-the-go breakfast muffins

They're muffins, Jim, but not as we know it! Forget your sugar-laden blueberry muffins in the morning (although they're great as a treat), these savoury muffins are like a moveable cooked breakfast. You can play around with any type of filling you want.

**MAKES 8**

olive oil, for greasing
  and cooking
8 large eggs
½ red onion, finely chopped
3-4 chestnut mushrooms,
  finely chopped
100g baby spinach
80g feta cheese, crumbled
  into pieces
5 slices Parma ham, sliced
sea salt

Preheat the oven to 180°C/350°F/Gas mark 4 and lightly oil 8 cups of a muffin tin.

Whisk the eggs in a bowl.

Heat a little olive oil in a pan and sauté the onion and mushrooms, with a little salt, until they are both soft and the mushrooms are releasing their juices. Add the spinach and continue to sauté until wilted.

Spoon the mixture and the crumbled feta into the oiled muffin cups and top up with the whisked egg, dividing it equally between them. Top with the ham and bake in the oven for about 18–20 minutes. Test by sticking in a fork – it should come out clean.

# Soups & starters

*Soups are a perfect way to create a dish that is incredibly nutrient-dense in a very small serving. By adding a diverse range of ingredients, you can cover a lot of nutritional bases. Get your oils right, too, and one simple soup can tick all of the three nutritional boxes. The starters here, whilst only being small plates, will still adhere to the Power of Three principles I recommend.*

## Balsamic baked apple and beetroot with whipped goat's cheese

**Balsamic baked apple and beetroot with whipped goat's cheese** This amazing dish is something I rustled up for one of my regular radio slots. The surprising combination makes for a decadent, satisfying starter.

**SERVES 2**

1 apple, cored and diced
2 large beetroots, washed
  and unpeeled, diced
2 tablespoons olive oil
2 tablespoons balsamic
  vinegar
150g soft goat's cheese
juice of ½ lemon

Preheat the oven to 200°C/400°F/Gas mark 6.

Place the diced apple and beetroot in a roasting tin. Drizzle with half the olive oil and half the balsamic vinegar. Stir well and roast in the oven for about 20 minutes.

Add the remaining balsamic vinegar, stir well and roast for a further 10–15 minutes.

Put the goat's cheese, lemon juice and remaining olive oil in a bowl and beat together using a spoon, whisk or similar, until it forms a smooth, cream-like texture.

Place a ring mould (about 7cm in diameter) in the centre of a plate and two-thirds fill it with the roasted apple and beetroot, pressing down well. Top with the whipped goat's cheese. Invert onto a plate before lifting the ring mould gently off to serve.

## Tomato seafood soup

Following my first trip to Rome not so long ago, I became hooked on the combination of rich tomato and seafood. It just has some kind of feelgood factor in taste and aroma. It also helps that combining these ingredients gives you a very broad spectrum of nutrients indeed.

**SERVES 2**
1 tablespoon olive oil
1 large red onion,
    finely chopped
2 cloves garlic, finely chopped
75g shelled mussels, plus
    extra shell-on mussels
    to serve (optional)
2–3 large, fresh squid tubes,
    cut into rings (including
    tentacles, if you like)
400g tomato passata
4–5 basil leaves, chopped
sea salt and black pepper

Heat the olive oil in a pan, add the onion and garlic with a pinch of salt and pepper, and sauté until the onion softens.

Add the mussels, squid rings and passata and simmer for about 15 minutes, until the seafood is cooked. Add the basil, stir and serve.

**Mighty miso soup** My many adventures in Japan have given me a taste for good miso soup. Over there, it is common to get a bowl of this wonderful stuff with all manner of vegetables and mushrooms in it – a far cry from the watery creation with a bit of seaweed floating in it that we so often get in restaurants here in the UK.

**SERVES 2**

¼ butternut squash,
   peeled, seeded and sliced
2 spring onions, sliced
   on the diagonal
4 shiitake mushrooms, sliced
1 tablespoon brown miso paste
100g firm tofu, cubed

Place 600ml water in a pan, add the sliced squash and spring onions and simmer for about 15 minutes, until the squash has softened.

Add the mushrooms and continue to simmer until they also begin to soften. Add the miso paste and dissolve by breaking the paste down against the side of the pan. Add the tofu, simmer for 1 minute, then serve.

# Cauliflower and cannellini soup

This great-tasting, creamy, filling soup is amazing in colder weather and has incredible nutrient density, and a very low GI.

**SERVES 2–3**

1 tablespoon olive oil
1 large white onion,
    finely chopped
2 cloves garlic, finely
    chopped
1 large cauliflower,
    broken into small florets
500ml vegetable stock
    (you may not need it all)
1 x 400g tin cannellini
    beans, drained
sea salt and black pepper

Heat the olive oil in a pan, add the onion and garlic with a pinch of salt, and sauté until the onion has softened.

Add the cauliflower and enough stock to almost cover the cauliflower. Simmer until the cauliflower is soft, then purée into a soup, using either a stick blender, food processor or jug blender.

Add the cannellini beans, put the soup back on the heat to warm through, then season to taste and serve.

## Smoked salmon parcels
This is a classic that never ages, and luckily fits all the criteria of this book too. Fresh, zesty and indulgent.

**SERVES 1**

3 tablespoons full-fat
    soft cheese
juice of ½ lemon
2 sprigs fresh dill,
    finely chopped
2 large slices
    smoked salmon
black pepper

Place the soft cheese, lemon juice, dill and some black pepper in a bowl and mix well.

Lay out the salmon slices and divide the cheese mixture evenly between them. Fold the edges of the salmon in towards the centre, creating parcels, and serve.

# Scallops with cumin cauliflower purée

The combination of scallops and cauliflower is a match made in heaven – the sweetness of the scallop with the gentle creaminess of the cauliflower creates magic. This is an immense hit of trace elements and potent phytochemicals, and is so fancy that you forget it's actually doing you good.

**SERVES 2**

olive oil, for cooking
1 white onion, finely chopped
1 clove garlic, finely chopped
1 small head of cauliflower,
   broken into florets
300ml vegetable stock
   (you may not need it all)
6 large scallops
2 small handfuls pea shoots
sea salt and black pepper

Heat a little olive oil in a pan, add the onion and garlic with a pinch of salt, and sauté until the onion has softened.

Add the cauliflower florets and enough stock to half cover the cauliflower. Simmer until the cauliflower has softened, then transfer to a blender or food processor and purée. The consistency should be like a thick soup.

Gently pan-fry the scallops in a small amount of olive oil for no more than 3 minutes on each side.

Place a dollop of purée in the centre of each serving plate, and spread out. Place 3 scallops on top of the purée, then top each with a small handful of pea shoots and a grinding of black pepper, and serve.

# Monkfish kebabs with avocado lime sauce

Here's a chance to try delicious monkfish for a starter, but of course you could use an alternative fish, like salmon, if you prefer.

**SERVES 2**

100g quinoa
2 teaspoons vegetable
   stock powder
2 monkfish fillets,
   skinned and diced
olive oil, to drizzle
2 tablespoons mixed
   seeds (e.g. sunflower,
   pumpkin and flax)
sea salt

**FOR THE SAUCE**

1 very ripe avocado
½ clove garlic, finely chopped
small bunch fresh coriander
   (about 1 tablespoon leaves)
juice of 2 limes
100ml water
2 teaspoons white miso paste

Place the quinoa in a pan and cover with boiling water. Add the stock powder and simmer for about 25 minutes until soft, and small tail-like projections begin to form on the grains. Drain, return to the pan and set aside.

Preheat the grill to high. Thread the diced fish onto 4 skewers and place on a baking tray. Drizzle with olive oil, add a pinch of salt and grill for about 12 minutes, turning regularly.

Blend all the sauce ingredients in a food processor to make a thick, smooth sauce.

Add the mixed seeds to the quinoa, warm the quinoa through, then divide between 2 plates. Serve with the skewers and the sauce.

# Tuna sashimi with pea shoots and wasabi avocado 'mayo'

This is a simple, indulgent treat. When you buy the tuna, make sure you get it from the fish counter, and please insist on stock that is fresh that day. If in any doubt, go without!

**SERVES 1**

¼ very ripe avocado
1 teaspoon wasabi
    (more if you like it hot)
1 tablespoon olive oil
juice of ¼ lemon
½ fresh tuna steak,
    cut into very fine slices
    (less than 5mm)
small handful pea shoots
finely chopped red chilli
    (optional)

Place the avocado, wasabi, olive oil and lemon juice in a food processor and process to a smooth, mayonnaise-like texture.

Lay the tuna slices along a plate. Top with the pea shoots and some chopped chilli, if you like, and serve with the avocado 'mayo'.

## Flax-coated calamari

**Flax-coated calamari** Calamari is absolutely one of my favourite things ever. I am quite partial to visiting the Mediterranean when I can, and calamari will usually be the first thing I order when I go out to eat. Squid are packed with zinc and selenium. The flax gives a lovely crunch.

**SERVES 2**
2 fresh squid tubes, plus
    baby squid if you like
5–6 tablespoons
    wholemeal flour
1 tablespoon ground flaxseeds
olive oil, for frying
lemon and/or lime wedges
sea salt and black pepper

Cut the squid tubes into rings.

Place the flour, ground flaxseeds and some salt and pepper in a plastic food bag and mix well.

Add the squid rings to the bag, seal the top and shake well for about 15 seconds, to ensure that all the rings are coated. Gently transfer the rings to a plate, one at a time, so as not to knock off too much of the coating.

Heat a 3cm depth of olive oil in a deep saucepan. Test the temperature by dropping a little bit of the flour mixture in – if it sizzles, it is ready.

Carefully lower the squid rings into the hot oil and fry for 3–4 minutes, until beginning to turn golden brown. Serve hot with lemon and/or lime wedges to squeeze over.

# King prawns with mango and chilli

This combination may sound a little unusual, but I got the idea from something I ate in Malaysia. I've just jazzed it up by using fresh mango rather than a processed mango sauce. This has the right balance of fresh and fiery.

**SERVES 1**

2 teaspoons coconut oil
2 spring onions,
    finely chopped
1 clove garlic, finely chopped
1 red chilli, finely sliced
½ ripe mango, peeled
    and diced
80g raw king prawns,
    peeled and deveined
small sprig fresh coriander,
    leaves torn
small handful rocket leaves
sea salt

Heat the coconut oil in a pan, add the spring onions, garlic and chilli with a pinch of salt, and sauté until the spring onions soften.

Add the mango and sauté for about 2 minutes. Add the king prawns and continue to cook, stirring, for about 3 minutes, or until fully pink all over.

Stir in the coriander and rocket and serve.

# Creamy mushrooms on oat flax galette

This is a lovely little starter – I adore mushrooms in any type of creamy sauce, and using soft cheese means you get more protein, which helps to keep you feeling fuller for longer.

**SERVES 1**

olive oil, for cooking
4–5 chestnut
   mushrooms, sliced
1 tablespoon soft cheese
1 egg
1 tablespoon oat bran
½ tablespoon
   ground flaxseeds
sea salt and cracked
   black pepper
small handful pea
   shoots, to serve

Heat a little olive oil in a pan, add the mushrooms, and sauté for 4–5 minutes, until cooked, soft and releasing some of their juices. Add the soft cheese and a generous amount of cracked black pepper.

Whisk the egg, oat bran and ground flaxseeds together in a bowl to form a batter, adding a little salt and pepper if desired.

Heat a little olive oil in a frying pan over a medium heat, add all the batter to make a small galette and fry for 3–4 minutes on each side, until golden.

Place the galette in the centre of a plate, spoon over the creamy mushrooms, then top with the pea shoots.

# Thai-style tuna and sweet potato fish cakes

Regular fish cakes do tend to be a total starch bomb and a very high GI affair, but using sweet potatoes and more fish than usual, with eggs too, creates a high-protein, slow-burning version that tastes insanely good. This is one recipe that kids seem to love too.

**SERVES 3–4**

300g sweet potato, peeled and diced
425g tinned tuna, drained
2 eggs, whisked
2 teaspoons Thai red curry paste
25g breadcrumbs
olive oil, for frying
sea salt

Place the diced sweet potato in a saucepan, cover with boiling water and simmer until soft. Drain, transfer to a bowl and set aside to cool.

When the potatoes are cool, add a good pinch of salt and mash. Add the tuna, eggs, Thai red curry paste and breadcrumbs, mix well and form into patties.

Heat some olive oil in a frying pan, add the patties and fry gently for about 4–5 minutes on each side, until crisp and golden. Serve with a side salad.

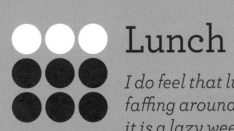

# Lunch

*I do feel that lunch should involve as little faffing around as possible, unless of course it is a lazy weekend. These recipes will deliver sound nutrition without all that time-consuming mucking about!*

# Beetroot, fig and feta salad with white vinaigrette

This is one of those glorious discoveries you make when using up leftovers in the fridge.

**SERVES 1**

2 handfuls mixed
   salad leaves
2 ripe figs, quartered
2 small cooked
   beetroot, quartered
100g feta cheese

**FOR THE DRESSING**

2 teaspoons white
   wine vinegar
1 tablespoon olive oil
½ teaspoon runny honey
sea salt and black pepper

Combine the salad leaves, figs and beetroot in a bowl. In a separate bowl, combine all the dressing ingredients and whisk well.

Dress the salad and toss well. Arrange on a plate, crumble the feta over the top and serve.

# Stir-fried greens with anchovies and poached eggs
This unusual combination has become one of my regular quick-fix staples when I am working from home and want something speedy but nutritious.

**SERVES 1**
2 large handfuls curly kale
2 cloves garlic, finely chopped
olive oil, for cooking
2 large eggs
5–6 anchovy fillets in oil
sea salt

Place the kale and garlic in a saucepan with a little olive oil and a pinch of salt, and sauté until the kale turns a brighter green and begins to soften a little.

Meanwhile, poach the eggs according to your own preference.

Place the kale in the centre of a plate. Scatter over the anchovy fillets and top with the poached eggs.

## Quicky chickpeas

Tinned pulses can be a lunchtime lifesaver. They provide a low-GI carbohydrate source, protein, B vitamins, and a few minerals to boot, and they're as fuss-free as you can get!

**SERVES 1**

olive oil, for cooking
1 large leek, thinly sliced
1 clove garlic, finely chopped
1 x 400g tin chickpeas, drained
¼ teaspoon ground cumin
½ teaspoon fennel seeds
sea salt

Heat a little olive oil, add the leek and garlic with a pinch of salt, and sauté until the leek softens.

Add the chickpeas, cumin and fennel seeds, mix well and cook for another 2–3 minutes, stirring frequently, until hot.

# Quinoa tabbouleh with avocado, olives and lemon flax dressing

This is a glorious summer salad, or a perfect winter side dish.

**SERVES 1**

50g quinoa
small bunch fresh parsley,
   very finely chopped
2 plum tomatoes,
   very finely diced
1 ripe avocado, diced
¼ red onion, finely diced
2 tablespoons pitted
   black olives, chopped
1 tablespoon flaxseed oil
finely grated zest of
   1 lemon and juice of ½
sea salt and black pepper

Place the quinoa in a saucepan, cover with boiling water and simmer for about 25 minutes until soft, and small tail-like projections form on the grains. Drain and set aside to dry for just a few minutes.

Tip the drained quinoa into a bowl and add the parsley, tomatoes, avocado, red onion and olives. Mix well and add pepper to taste.

Combine the flaxseed oil, lemon zest and juice with salt and pepper to taste, and whisk to form a dressing. Dress the quinoa mixture and toss well before serving.

## Warm chicken liver salad

This classic combo is a real nutrient fest. Offal is still rather unpopular these days, but it is one of the richest sources of nutrients, such as the B vitamins, vitamin A and many minerals. There are few foods that even come close when it comes to nutrient density.

**SERVES 1**
olive oil, for cooking
½ red onion, thinly sliced
2–3 slices fennel bulb
50g chicken livers
1 large handful mixed
    baby leaves
sea salt

Heat a little olive oil in a pan, add the onion and fennel with a pinch of salt, and sauté until soft.

Add the chicken livers and cook for about 6–7 minutes, until nicely browning on the outside and cooked through.

Place the salad leaves in the centre of a plate, add the liver, onion and fennel mixture and toss together before serving.

# Mushroom topped with spinach, sun-dried tomatoes and goat's cheese, with kale salad This is such a gorgeous lunch with plenty of flavour and a wonderful Mediterranean vibe.

**SERVES 1**

1 handful baby spinach
1 large, flat field mushroom
olive oil, for cooking
3 sun-dried tomatoes, diced
1 slice goat's cheese, 1cm thick

**FOR THE SALAD**

2 handfuls curly kale,
    thick stems removed
1 tablespoon olive oil,
    plus extra to drizzle
1 teaspoon balsamic vinegar
1 small clove garlic,
    finely chopped
sea salt and black pepper

Preheat the oven to 160°C/325°F/Gas mark 3.

Put the spinach and 2 teaspoons water in a pan and steam-sauté for just long enough for the leaves to wilt.

Gently fry the whole mushroom on each side in a little olive oil, until both sides are beginning to moisten as the mushroom releases some of its juices. Transfer to a baking tray, gill-side up. Fill with the wilted spinach, then add the sun-dried tomatoes and top with the slice of goat's cheese. Bake in the oven just until the goat's cheese has melted – keep an eye on it!

Place the kale in a bowl. Drizzle with a little olive oil and a pinch of salt, then massage into the kale until wilted. Whisk together the vinegar, olive oil and garlic and season to taste with pepper. Dress the kale before plating up with the mushroom.

# Peppery chickpea, beetroot and orange salad

This lovely, refreshing salad offers punchy pepperiness, sweetness and freshness. Packed with minerals and B vitamins.

**SERVES 1**

1 x 200g tin chickpeas, drained
1 large handful rocket leaves
1 large handful watercress
1 cooked beetroot, cut into wedges
½ orange, segmented

**FOR THE DRESSING**

1 teaspoon piccalilli
1 tablespoon olive oil
pinch ground cumin

Place the chickpeas, rocket, watercress and beetroot in a bowl and mix well.

Whisk the dressing ingredients together, dress the salad and toss well, then add the orange segments and serve.

## Peppered mackerel with capers, cucumber and yoghurt, with rocket on rye

This is a great open sandwich, with the contrast of the strong flavours from the peppered mackerel combining with the cooling yoghurt; a lovely dish for an al fresco lunch.

**SERVES 1**

1 peppered smoked mackerel
   fillet, flaked
2 tablespoons natural yoghurt
1 teaspoon capers
2.5cm piece cucumber, diced
1 slice rye bread
small handful rocket leaves
sea salt

Place the flaked mackerel, yoghurt, capers and cucumber in a bowl, add a small pinch of salt and mix well.

Place the mixture on the rye bread and top with the rocket leaves.

# Roasted sweet potato salad with pine nuts and green power dressing

This wonderful salad does take a little more prepping but is completely worth it. The dressing delivers a sweet, creamy, zingy flavour that turns it from a light meal into a substantial nutrient fest!

**SERVES 1**
½ medium unpeeled sweet
    potato, cut into slim wedges
1 tablespoon olive oil
2 handfuls mixed salad leaves
1 tablespoon pine nuts

**FOR THE DRESSING**
½ ripe avocado
small bunch fresh coriander
5–6 fresh basil leaves
juice of ½ lime
½ teaspoon runny honey
100ml water
sea salt and black pepper

Preheat the oven to 200°C/400°F/Gas mark 6.

Place the sweet potato in a roasting tin, drizzle with the olive oil and roast in the oven for about 25 minutes, until the edges are turning a golden brown and the flesh is soft.

Place all the dressing ingredients in a blender or food processor, with salt and pepper to taste, and blend to a thick, bright green dressing.

Mix the salad leaves with the sweet potato and pine nuts and top with the dressing.

# Courgette ribbon and fennel salad with honey mustard dressing

Courgette ribbons are a great alternative to noodles, as many of the commonly available noodles have a very high glycaemic impact and can play havoc with blood sugar. When marinated briefly, courgette noodles take on a tagliatelle-like vibe.

**SERVES 1**
1 large courgette
2 teaspoons olive oil
½ large fennel bulb,
    cut into matchsticks

**FOR THE DRESSING**
1 teaspoon wholegrain
    mustard
1 teaspoon runny honey
1 tablespoon olive oil

Using a swivel vegetable peeler, slice the courgette lengthways into thin ribbons. Put into a bowl, drizzle over the olive oil, toss well and leave to marinate for 1–2 hours.

Add the fennel sticks to the marinated courgette and mix well.

Combine the dressing ingredients and whisk. Pour the dressing over the courgette and fennel and toss well to coat.

# Chicken, avocado and blue cheese salad

This is a firm favourite of mine, a salad that is popular around California and one of the first things on my list whenever I visit. This really does encompass each principle in this book: amazing nutrient density, very low glycaemic response and rich in fatty acids...Oh, and it tastes amazing too!

**SERVES 1**

2 handfuls mixed
  salad leaves
1 cooked chicken
  breast, sliced
½ ripe avocado, sliced
60g blue cheese, diced
  or crumbled
1–2 soft- or hard-boiled
  eggs, halved or chopped

**FOR THE DRESSING**

2 teaspoons mayonnaise
3 teaspoons olive oil
1 teaspoon white
  wine vinegar
1 teaspoon grated
  Parmesan cheese

Place the mixed leaves in a bowl and top with the chicken, avocado, blue cheese and soft- or hard-boiled eggs.

Combine the dressing ingredients and mix well, before pouring over the salad and tossing well to coat.

## Avocado, roasted tomato and green bean salad This is a lovely main-course salad, or can be just as at home served as a side. You could also jazz it up with some fresh buffalo mozzarella.

**SERVES 2**

4 plum tomatoes or
   handful baby plum
   tomatoes, halved
140g green beans,
   ends trimmed
1 ripe avocado, sliced
1 handful baby spinach
sea salt and black pepper

**FOR THE DRESSING**

juice of ½ lemon
1 tablespoon olive oil
½ clove garlic,
   finely chopped

Preheat the oven to 180°C/350°F/Gas mark 4.

Place the tomato halves cut side up on a baking tray and sprinkle with a little salt. Roast in the oven for 15–30 minutes (depending on their size), until beginning to shrivel. Remove and set aside.

Place the green beans in a saucepan, cover with boiling water and simmer for 5–10 minutes until they have turned a brighter green and softer, but still have a little bite. Drain and tip into a bowl.

Add the avocado, roasted tomatoes and baby spinach to the beans.

Combine the dressing ingredients, with salt and pepper to taste, and whisk to emulsify. Dress the salad and toss well before serving.

# Niçoise lettuce wraps Here is a slightly different way to enjoy one of my all-time top salads. This is a good option for at-desk dining!

**SERVES 1**

1 x 112g tin tuna, drained
1 tablespoon mayonnaise
1 teaspoon capers
juice of ½ lemon
3 large lettuce leaves
6 anchovy fillets in oil
9 pitted black olives, chopped
4–6 cherry tomatoes, halved
sea salt and black pepper

Place the tuna, mayonnaise, capers, lemon juice and a pinch of salt and pepper in a bowl and mix well.

Lay out the lettuce leaves facing up, to form little cups. Divide the tuna mixture between them.

Place 2 anchovy fillets, 3 olives and 3–4 cherry tomato halves in each lettuce cup, before rolling up into a wrap.

## Trout and asparagus crustless quiche

**Trout and asparagus crustless quiche** I used to be obsessed with my mum's quiches. They are so, SO good. These days I am a bit of a pastry dodger, unless it's a special occasion. A crustless quiche is the way to go if you want to keep it really low-GI. Plus it is a whole lot quicker to make!

**SERVES 3–4**

olive oil, for greasing
55g cooked asparagus spears
2 cooked trout fillets, flaked
3 large eggs plus 3 large
   egg whites
170ml milk
2 tablespoons grated
   Parmesan cheese
small sprinkle of grated
   cheese (optional)
sea salt and black pepper

Preheat the oven to 180°C/350°F/Gas mark 4.

Lightly oil a 23cm diameter baking or tart dish. Scatter the asparagus and flaked trout evenly across the base.

Whisk the whole eggs, egg whites, milk, Parmesan and some salt and pepper together in a bowl or jug.

Pour the egg mixture over the trout and asparagus, sprinkle with the grated cheese and bake in the oven for about 45 minutes, or until the centre no longer wobbles. Leave to cool completely before serving.

**Speedy beef stir-fry** This is a great warm lunch that doesn't take long to cook at all, and is rich and hearty. Chinese chilli bean sauce is available in almost every supermarket these days. Serve as it is or with a very small amount of cooked brown rice.

**SERVES 1**
olive oil, for stir-frying
3 spring onions, cut on the
  diagonal into 1cm pieces
2 cloves garlic, finely sliced
1 small steak, cut into
  thin strips
1 handful curly kale
1 handful baby spinach
1 teaspoon runny honey
2 teaspoons soy sauce
2 teaspoons toasted sesame oil
2 teaspoons chilli bean sauce
sea salt

Heat a little olive oil in a pan, add the spring onions and garlic with a pinch of salt, and sauté until the spring onions begin to soften. Add the beef strips and stir-fry for 6 minutes.

Add the greens and stir-fry for 3 minutes. Add the honey, soy sauce, sesame oil and chilli bean sauce, mix well, and cook for another minute before serving.

# Prawn and avocado wrap with almond chilli dipping sauce

This is another winner for me. The flavour of the dipping sauce is off the scale! To be honest I could just sit and eat the sauce with a spoon – it's that good! The creamy, cooling avocado balances out some of the fire from the sauce.

**SERVES 1**

1 wholemeal tortilla wrap
½ very ripe avocado, mashed
75g cooked king prawns
small sprig fresh coriander
sea salt and black pepper
   (optional)

**FOR THE SAUCE**

2 tablespoons almond butter
2 teaspoons soy sauce
1 teaspoon runny honey
1 clove garlic, finely chopped
1 small red chilli, finely
   chopped
3–4 tablespoons water

Place all the sauce ingredients in a bowl and mix gently to bring the water and the other ingredients together – you will struggle to mix them at first but they suddenly come together after a minute or so. The consistency should be smooth but not too thick.

Lay the tortilla out flat and spoon the mashed avocado across the centre. Add a little salt and pepper if desired. Place the prawns and coriander on top of the mashed avocado, then roll up tightly.

Cut across the middle to give you two halves, then dip away! If you are a neater eater, dollop the sauce over the filling before rolling up the tortilla wrap.

## Smoked trout, cucumber and tzatziki sourdough open sandwich

This has a lovely refreshing flavour to it, and it feels as though you should be serving it with some afternoon tea. It's got that kind of vibe, or maybe that's just me! Great with a side salad.

**SERVES 1**

1 slice sourdough bread, toasted
6–7 thin slices cucumber
2 slices smoked trout, flaked
small sprig fresh dill, torn

**FOR THE TZATZIKI**

1 tablespoon plain yoghurt
2-cm piece of cucumber, grated
6–7 mint leaves, roughly chopped
sea salt and black pepper

To make the tzatziki, mix together all the ingredients and season with a small pinch of salt and pepper.

Then simply layer up on the toast as follows: cucumber slices, then smoked trout, then tzatziki, then dill.

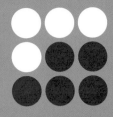

# Dinner

*All these dishes serve 1, as I find this
an easier way to present my recipes.
Just multiply any recipe by however
many people you're cooking for.
It's as simple as that!*

## Broccoli, fig and anchovy pizza with fresh rocket

I do love a good pizza, and this is a beautiful flavour combination – sweet, salty, peppery, earthy. So many things going on at once. It's just a total bargain that the nutrient density is top notch too!

**SERVES 1**
250g wholemeal flour
1 teaspoon dried yeast
2 tablespoons olive oil,
    plus extra to drizzle
125ml warm water

**FOR THE TOPPING**
1 tablespoon tomato passata
4–5 mozzarella slices
6–7 steamed broccoli
    florets, halved
2 ripe figs, sliced
4–6 anchovy fillets in oil,
    chopped
1 handful rocket leaves
sea salt and black pepper

Combine the flour, yeast, olive oil and water in a bowl and mix well to form a dough. Turn the dough out onto a clean work surface and knead – the technique doesn't really matter, just get the dough moving for a couple of minutes. Return to the bowl, cover and leave for 30 minutes. Meanwhile, preheat the oven to 200°C/400°F/Gas mark 6.

Roll the dough out to a round about 30cm in diameter and place on a pizza tray or large baking tray. Drizzle with olive oil. Bake in the oven for about 10–12 minutes, until firming and there is the slightest trace of it turning golden.

Remove from the oven and spread the passata over the base. Arrange a couple of slices of the mozzarella. Dot the broccoli around, arrange the fig slices and anchovies, then add the remaining mozzarella, along with a pinch of salt and pepper.

Return to the oven for about 8 minutes, until the mozzarella is bubbling in the middle and developing brown bubbles around the edges. Remove from the oven and top with the rocket.

# Salmon, prawn and fennel spaghetti

This is an indulgent and creamy dish that is actually far lighter than it appears. Pasta can sometimes be troublesome for blood sugar but this wholewheat version, coupled with this amount of protein, has a much lower impact on blood sugar.

**SERVES 1**

75g wholewheat spaghetti
   or linguine
olive oil, for cooking
¼ white onion, sliced
½ fennel bulb, sliced
1 salmon fillet, skinned
   and diced
90g raw king prawns
1 heaped tablespoon
   soft cheese
small sprig fresh dill,
   chopped
sea salt

Place the pasta in a saucepan and pour boiling water over it to cover. Simmer for about 15 minutes, until softened but it still retains a little bite, then drain.

Meanwhile, heat a little olive oil in a pan, add the onion and fennel with a pinch of salt, and sauté until the onion is slightly transparent and the fennel begins to soften. Add the salmon and prawns and sauté for 6–8 minutes until both are cooked.

Add the soft cheese, dill and 2 tablespoons water. Tip in the drained pasta and combine well before serving.

## Mackerel with barlotto bianco and green sauce

Barlotto bianco is a healthy incarnation of a classic white risotto, using pearl barley for a serious slow burn!

**SERVES 1**
olive oil, for cooking
½ white onion,
    finely chopped
1 large clove garlic,
    finely chopped
125g pearl barley
500ml vegetable stock
1 fresh mackerel fillet

**FOR THE SAUCE**
½ ripe avocado
1 clove garlic
1 teaspoon capers
1 handful flat-leaf
    parsley leaves
small sprig fresh
    coriander
small sprig fresh basil
½ spring onion
juice of ½ lime
sea salt and
    black pepper

Heat a little olive oil in a pan, add the onion and garlic with a pinch of salt, and sauté until the onion has softened.

Add the pearl barley and a small amount of stock and simmer until the stock is absorbed. Keep adding the stock in increments until the barley has softened – pearl barley requires much more liquid than regular risotto rice. This will take around 30 minutes or more.

Place all the sauce ingredients in a food processor, with salt and pepper to taste, and blend. Add enough water, a little at a time, for it to turn into a thick, smooth sauce (you should have about 100ml in total). Transfer the sauce to a pan and set aside.

Gently pan-fry the mackerel for about 5 minutes on each side. You can do it for a little less, but I think a little bit of crispiness on the edges is a lovely touch. Gently warm through the sauce over a low heat.

Spoon the barlotto into the centre of a serving plate. Place the mackerel fillet on top, then drizzle the sauce over it.

# Steak with beetroot and goat's cheese mash and red onion gravy

Ok, ok this sounds a little...unusual! This idea came to me one night when I was lying in bed and couldn't sleep. I tried it the very next day and the flavour sensation was unbelievable.

**SERVES 1**
1 sirloin steak
olive oil, for cooking
1 red onion, halved
   and sliced
1 teaspoon plain flour
25ml red wine
100ml beef stock
2 medium-sized
   cooked beetroot
75g soft goat's cheese
sea salt and black pepper

Cook the steak according to your preference.

Meanwhile, heat a little olive oil in a pan, add the red onion and sauté until soft. Add the flour, stir well, then add the red wine and beef stock and simmer, stirring, to get rid of any lumps, until it reaches a thicker consistency.

Mash the beetroot using a potato masher – it won't be as smooth as mash, but not far off. Add the goat's cheese with a pinch of salt and pepper and mix well. Transfer the mixture to a saucepan and warm through.

Plate up the mash, put the steak on top, then smother with the gravy. It would be great served with some cooked greens.

## Chicken escalope

**Chicken escalope** I hate to admit it, but as a kid I was partial to some of the nasty breaded chicken-type monstrosities. I wouldn't touch them with a barge pole now, but I have found a way to get that whole escalope/schnitzel vibe without it being riddled with junk.

**SERVES 1**

1 large boneless, skinless chicken breast
1 tablespoon fine oatmeal
2 teaspoons ground flaxseeds
¼ teaspoon garlic powder or granules
pinch of sea salt and black pepper

Preheat the oven to 190°C/375°F/Gas mark 5.

Place the chicken breast in a freezer bag, or sandwich it between two layers of cling film. Using a rolling pin or other suitable blunt instrument, gently bash the chicken to flatten it out to about a thickness between 1 and 1.5cm. Discard the bag or cling film.

Combine the oatmeal, ground flaxseeds, garlic, salt and pepper in a bowl and mix well. Transfer the flattened chicken to the bowl and toss it over and over to ensure that it gets thoroughly coated in the mixture.

Place the coated chicken breast flat on a baking tray and bake in the oven for about 25 minutes, or until crispy and turning golden; keep an eye on it.

Serve with a mixed leaf salad and some sweet potato wedges.

# Sesame salmon with miso aubergine and gingered greens

Whilst travelling through Japan I discovered a small, traditional restaurant in the Kansai region. I was served dozens of little healthy dishes, one of which was heavenly aubergine cooked in miso. I have since seen it on menus in trendy Asian fusion restaurants in the UK.

**SERVES 1**

3 teaspoons soy sauce
3 teaspoons toasted
    sesame oil
2 teaspoons runny honey
1 large salmon fillet
olive oil, for greasing
    and cooking
½ aubergine, thinly sliced
1 tablespoon brown miso paste
large handful shredded greens
1cm piece fresh ginger,
    peeled and sliced
    into matchsticks
1 teaspoon sesame seeds

Put the soy sauce, sesame oil and honey in a bowl and mix well. Place the salmon fillet in the mixture and toss it over several times to ensure a good coating. Marinate for 2–3 hours, turning the salmon occasionally.

Preheat the oven to 200°C/400°F/Gas mark 6.

Lift the salmon out of the marinade and onto an oiled baking tray. Spoon most of the marinade over it, reserving a drizzle in the bowl. Bake the salmon for 12–15 minutes (I like it a little pink still, but go up to 20 minutes if you prefer).

Heat a little olive oil in a pan, add the aubergine slices and sauté until soft. Add the miso paste and mix well.

Sauté the greens in a little olive oil until beginning to soften and wilt, then add the ginger and sauté until nice and soft.

Plate the greens, aubergine and salmon, then drizzle the reserved marinade over the salmon. Sprinkle with the sesame seeds, then serve.

# Spinach seafood pancakes

These funky-coloured pancakes make dinner a little different. You can get creative with the greens too – try adding some fresh coriander or dill. Even some chilli!

**MAKES UP TO 4 PANCAKES**

100g spinach
125g plain wholemeal flour
450ml milk
1 egg
olive oil, for cooking
1 clove garlic, chopped
150g cooked prawns
125g cooked salmon
    fillet, flaked
1 tablespoon soft cheese
juice of ½ lemon,
    plus wedges to serve
1 tablespoon chopped
    parsley (optional)
sea salt

Place the spinach and 1 tablespoon water in a saucepan. Set over a high heat and steam-sauté until it wilts. Using the back of a spoon, give it a squeeze to get as much liquid out as possible, then transfer to a food processor with the flour, milk and egg. Whizz to a smooth batter.

Heat a little olive oil in a saucepan, add the garlic and sauté for 2–3 minutes. Add the prawns, flaked salmon and soft cheese and cook for 3 minutes. Remove from the heat and leave to cool slightly, then stir in the lemon juice.

Heat a little olive oil in a 20cm frying pan and add enough pancake batter to cover the base of the pan. Cook for 1–1½ minutes until the underside is turning golden brown and easily lifts away from the pan. Gently flip and cook for another minute. Repeat to use up the mixture and make more pancakes.

Place each pancake on a plate, spoon over the prawn and salmon mixture and scatter with the parsley, if using. Wrap up and serve with lemon wedges and a salad.

## Pasta puttanesca
This lovely pasta sauce has several variations throughout Italy, and this is my preferred one.
I do tend to go slightly heavier on the anchovies just to get that additional omega-3 hit in!

**SERVES 1**
olive oil, for cooking
2 cloves garlic,
    finely chopped
6 anchovy fillets
    in oil, halved
1 tablespoon pitted
    black olives
1 teaspoon capers
1 x 200g tin chopped
    tomatoes
80g wholewheat penne
black pepper

Heat a little olive oil in a pan, add the garlic and sauté for about 2 minutes. Add the anchovies, olives and capers, and sauté for another 2 minutes. Add the tomatoes and simmer for 10–12 minutes. Add pepper to taste.

Meanwhile, cook the pasta in simmering water until soft but with a little bite remaining. Drain, then add to the sauce, stirring well to combine.

# River cobbler with coriander cashew crust on Asian soba noodle salad

This is a divine, flavoursome treat – packed with zing and showcasing some really nutrient-dense ingredients. The noodle salad is served cold here, but you could easily warm it through, or stir-fry the vegetables first before adding the noodles and seasonings.

**SERVES 1**

2 tablespoons cashew nuts
small bunch fresh coriander
1 small clove garlic, peeled
2 teaspoons olive oil,
    plus extra for greasing
1 river cobbler fillet
75g dried soba noodles
1 carrot, grated
1 spring onion, halved and
    sliced into matchsticks
½ red chilli, sliced
2 teaspoons sesame oil
2 teaspoons soy sauce
1 teaspoon runny honey

Preheat the oven to 190°C/375°F/Gas mark 5.

Place the cashews, coriander, garlic and olive oil in a food processor and pulse to a coarse pesto-like texture.

Place the river cobbler fillet on an oiled baking sheet, transfer to the oven and cook for about 12 minutes. Remove from the oven, smother the cashew and coriander mixture on top and return to the oven for 15–20 minutes, until the crust is beginning to firm up and is slightly crisp around the edges.

Meanwhile, cook the soba noodles in simmering water for 4–5 minutes, or until they soften and reach a cooked pasta texture. Drain and rinse in cold water.

Place the noodles in a bowl with the carrot, spring onion, chilli, sesame oil, soy sauce and honey, and toss well. Serve topped with the baked fish.

## Tofu, courgette and shiitake mushrooms in squash sauce

This is a serious nutrient injection and flavour bomb. The beauty is that you can vary the ingredients as much as you like – I just think tofu and aubergine work particularly well. I got this idea from resurrecting some leftover soup.

**SERVES 1–2**

olive or coconut oil,
    for cooking
1 red onion, finely chopped
2 cloves garlic, finely chopped
½ small butternut squash,
    seeded and diced
300ml vegetable stock
1 large courgette, sliced
    into rounds
1 small punnet shiitake
    mushrooms, sliced
large handful baby spinach
170g firm tofu, diced
sea salt and black pepper

Heat a little olive or coconut oil in a pan, add the onion and garlic and sauté with a pinch of salt, until the onion is soft.

Add the diced squash and enough vegetable stock to just cover the squash. Simmer until the squash is nice and soft, then transfer to a food processor or blender and blend to a thick, silky consistency. Season with pepper to taste.

Sauté the courgette and mushrooms in a little olive or coconut oil until they are nice and soft. Add the spinach and sauté until wilted.

Pour in the squash sauce and add the diced tofu. Simmer for a couple of minutes until the tofu has warmed through, then serve with brown rice or some steamed greens.

## Thai-style duck curry
I'm a real sucker for Thai flavours, and I do love game meats too, so this dish is a sure-fire hit in my house. It can be served with brown rice, quinoa or, as I often have it, with some cooked greens.

**SERVES 1**

½ red onion,
   roughly chopped
½ red chilli (more if
   you want), chopped
1 large clove garlic,
   roughly chopped
1cm piece fresh ginger,
   peeled and chopped
1 lemongrass stalk,
   bashed then chopped
1 handful fresh coriander
   leaves, torn, plus extra
   to serve
3 fresh basil leaves
1 teaspoon ground coriander
1 teaspoon fish sauce
juice of ¼ lime
coconut or olive oil,
   for cooking
200ml coconut milk
100ml vegetable stock
1 duck breast (skin on),
   cut into bite-sized pieces

Place the red onion, chilli, garlic, ginger, lemongrass, coriander and basil leaves, ground coriander, fish sauce and lime juice in a food processor and blitz to a smooth paste.

Heat a little coconut or olive oil in a saucepan, add the paste and fry until it turns a notably darker colour and becomes less pungent.

Add the coconut milk and stock, stir well and simmer for about 5 minutes. Add the chopped duck breast and simmer for another 10–12 minutes.

Serve with extra coriander leaves.

# Chicken stuffed with kale and goat's cheese, with citrus omega salad

This is a really satisfying dish. I've always loved chicken with something creamy, and a nice, rich goat's cheese is the perfect partner here.

**SERVES 1**
1 handful curly kale
50g soft goat's cheese
1 large boneless, skinless
    chicken breast
1 handful mixed salad leaves
½ orange, peeled, pith
    removed, segmented

**FOR THE DRESSING**
1 tablespoon flaxseed oil
1 tablespoon orange juice
2 teaspoons soy sauce

Preheat the oven to 200°C/400°F/Gas mark 6.

Blanch the kale in boiling water for 1–2 minutes, then drain and plunge straight into a bowl of cold water to refresh. Drain thoroughly and chop, then mix well with the goat's cheese.

Slice along one side of the chicken breast, about halfway up, to create a pocket. Spoon in the kale and goat's cheese mixture, then close the pocket up. Try to wrap a small piece of the upper or lower part of the breast over the cut, to create a seal, then place a couple of cocktail sticks through the seal to hold it in place. Place the chicken on a baking tray and bake in the oven for 20–25 minutes.

Place the salad leaves on a serving plate and scatter the orange segments over it.

Combine the dressing ingredients and whisk well to make an emulsion. Slice the chicken breast into several slices and arrange over the centre of the plate. Pour the dressing over the chicken and salad, then serve.

**Omega curry** This delightful dish came about because I asked an Indian restaurant I know well to combine two dishes from their menu – salmon tikka and dhansak. The result was epic! Here is a simple make-at-home version. Serve with Rainbow Rice (page 156) or Chana Saag (page 158).

**SERVES 1**

1 large salmon fillet
  (skin on or off)
1 teaspoon mild tandoori paste
olive or coconut oil,
  for cooking
½ red onion, finely chopped
1 clove garlic, finely chopped
1 teaspoon ground turmeric
¼ teaspoon ground cumin
¼ teaspoon ground coriander
½ teaspoon ground cinnamon
120g red lentils
4 pitted dates, finely chopped
250ml vegetable stock
small bunch fresh coriander,
  coarsely chopped
sea salt

Preheat the oven to 200°C/400°F/Gas mark 6.

Place the salmon on a baking tray and spread the tandoori paste over it. (Oil the tray first if the salmon has its skin, and arrange it skin down.) Bake in the oven for about 20 minutes.

Meanwhile, heat a little olive or coconut oil in a pan, add the onion and garlic with a pinch of salt, and sauté until the onion has softened. Add the turmeric, cumin, ground coriander and cinnamon and sauté for 2–3 minutes.

Add the lentils, dates and a small amount of the vegetable stock. Simmer until the stock has begun to be absorbed by the lentils, then add more stock, and continue this process, as you would for making risotto. Once the curry has reached a thick gravy-like texture, stir in the chopped coriander.

Place the salmon on a serving plate and pour the lentil curry over the top.

# Baked aubergine with tahini sauce

I took inspiration for this dish from the wonderful Yotam Ottolenghi. The flavours are magical and create such a dense, low-GI nutritional cocktail.

**SERVES 1**

½ large aubergine, cut lengthways, flesh scored in a criss-cross fashion
olive oil, to drizzle
1 teaspoon pomegranate seeds
sea salt

**FOR THE SAUCE**

1 tablespoon tahini
1 small clove garlic, finely chopped
¼ teaspoon ground cumin
juice of ½ lemon

Preheat the oven to 200°C/400°F/Gas mark 6.

Place the aubergine scored side up on a baking tray, drizzle with a little olive oil and add a pinch of salt. Bake in the oven for about 30 minutes, moving it around occasionally to stop it catching on the tray.

Combine the sauce ingredients in a bowl. Spoon the sauce over the baked aubergine and sprinkle over the pomegranate seeds. Serve with a side salad, sautéed greens or roasted red peppers and courgettes.

# Aubergine cannelloni with walnut pesto on rich tomato sauce

This is an awesome comfort dish. I used to love cannelloni, but I can generally do without the starch overload, so this is a great way to get a similar deal without sending your blood sugar through the roof.

**SERVES 1**

3 long, 0.5–1cm-thick slices
   from 1 large aubergine
olive oil, for brushing
   and cooking

**FOR THE TOMATO SAUCE**

½ red onion, finely chopped
1 clove garlic, finely chopped
200g tomato passata
1 teaspoon dried oregano

**FOR THE PESTO**

5 tablespoons walnuts
25g fresh basil leaves
2 cloves garlic,
   finely chopped
3 teaspoons grated
   Parmesan cheese
1½ tablespoons olive oil
sea salt and black pepper

Preheat the oven to 180°C/350°F/Gas mark 4.

Brush the aubergine slices on both sides with olive oil and place on a non-stick baking tray. Bake in the oven (or griddle on a hot griddle pan) for about 20 minutes, or until golden on both sides and soft enough to roll, but not so soft they will fall apart.

For the tomato sauce, heat a little olive oil in a pan, add the onion and garlic with a pinch of salt, and sauté until the onion softens. Add the passata and oregano and simmer for 12–15 minutes.

Meanwhile, place all the pesto ingredients in a food processor, with salt and pepper to taste, and pulse to create a coarse pesto.

Place a generous dollop of pesto in the centre of each aubergine slice, then roll up. Warm in the oven for a few minutes. Heat through the tomato sauce, then ladle it onto the serving plate and place the cannelloni on top of the sauce.

# Salmon and spinach filo parcel

This is a lovely, lighter version of salmon *en croûte* that can be a great quick-fix meal if you use ready-cooked salmon fillets.

**SERVES 1**
large handful baby spinach
2 tablespoons soft cheese
2 teaspoons chopped
   fresh dill
3 sheets filo pastry
1 cooked salmon fillet
olive oil, for greasing
sea salt and cracked
   black pepper

Preheat the oven to 180°C/350°F/Gas mark 4.

Put the spinach and 1 tablespoon water in a saucepan. Place over a high heat and stir until the steam from the water wilts the spinach. Add the soft cheese and dill, season to taste and mix well.

Brush each filo sheet with olive oil and lay one on top of the other. Dollop the spinach mixture into the middle. Pull the salmon flesh from the skin in chunks, and place these on top of the spinach mixture. Wrap the sides of the filo over the top of the filling to create a parcel.

Place the parcel on an oiled baking tray and bake in the oven for 20 minutes, or until the filo is golden and crispy. Serve with sweet potato wedges and a salad.

# White fish with peppered mushroom topping on courgettes and broad beans

This is a simple throw-together dinner that I often call on. Simple, fresh flavours. You can use any white fish – it works well with cod, sea bass or even river cobbler.

**SERVES 1**
1 cod fillet (or white
   fish of your choice)
olive oil, for greasing
   and cooking
4–5 chestnut
   mushrooms, sliced
1 sprig fresh rosemary
1 tablespoon soft cheese
knob of butter
1 small courgette, sliced
200g broad beans
   (drain them if tinned)
sea salt and cracked
   black pepper

Preheat the oven to 200°C/400°F/Gas mark 6.

Place the fish on an oiled baking tray and bake in the oven for about 20 minutes.

Meanwhile, heat a little olive oil in a pan, add the mushrooms and rosemary with a pinch of salt, and sauté. When the mushrooms start to release their juices, simmer for about 8 minutes for the rosemary to infuse its flavour into the juices. Discard the rosemary, then stir in the soft cheese, along with a generous amount of cracked black pepper.

Melt the butter with a little more olive oil in a pan, add the courgette and broad beans and sauté until the courgette is soft. Season to taste.

Place the courgette and broad bean mixture in the centre of a serving plate. Place the fish on top, then smother with the mushrooms.

# Tilapia with mustard sauce, kale and roasted celeriac

This brings together some gorgeous flavours that make a warming winter treat. The celeriac could also work very well as a mash.

**SERVES 1**

¼ large celeriac,
    peeled and diced
olive oil, for cooking
1 tilapia fillet
2 handfuls curly kale

**FOR THE SAUCE**

2 tablespoons Greek yoghurt
1 teaspoon runny honey
juice of ½ lemon
1 teaspoon wholegrain
    mustard
2 teaspoons chopped chives
½ clove garlic, very
    finely chopped
2 teaspoons boiling water
sea salt and black pepper

Preheat the oven to 200°C/400°F/Gas mark 6.

Place the diced celeriac in a roasting tin, drizzle with a little olive oil and roast in the oven for about 25 minutes, until soft and the edges are becoming crispy.

Gently fry the tilapia fillet in a little olive oil for about 10 minutes, turning frequently, until the edges turn golden and begin to crisp.

Meanwhile, steam the curly kale for 6–8 minutes, until it turns a brighter green and softens.

Combine the sauce ingredients in a bowl, with salt and pepper to taste, and mix well.

Place the celeriac and kale on a plate, top with the tilapia and drizzle over the sauce.

# Nutty sweet potato stew This has a nicely satisfying texture and a surprisingly comforting flavour.

**SERVES 1**

40g peanuts
olive oil, for cooking
½ red onion, finely chopped
1 clove garlic, finely chopped
1 teaspoon cumin seeds
100g unpeeled sweet
   potato, diced
100g tinned chopped tomatoes
1 handful baby spinach
sea salt

Place the peanuts in a folded tea towel and give them a bash with a rolling pin to crush them.

Heat a little olive oil in a pan, add the onion and garlic with a pinch of salt, and sauté until the onion is soft. Add the cumin seeds and sauté for 2 minutes. Add the sweet potato and tomatoes and simmer for about 15 minutes. Add the crushed peanuts and simmer for another 15 minutes.

At the last minute, add the spinach and check the seasoning before serving.

# Slow-burn paella
This is a very low-GI version of the Spanish classic. I'm obsessed with shellfish, especially squid, and this is a great way to introduce people to these ingredients. This dish encompasses every principle in this book: nutrient-dense, rich in omega-3 fatty acids, and it will drip-feed blood sugar for hours. I have added turmeric here in place of saffron, just for an additional antioxidant kick, but feel free to stick to saffron if you like.

**SERVES 1**

olive oil, for cooking
½ red onion, finely chopped
1 clove garlic, finely chopped
25g cooking chorizo, sliced
½ teaspoon ground turmeric
¼ teaspoon paprika
60g short-grain brown rice
300ml vegetable stock
2 fresh squid tubes, sliced
   into rings or strips, plus
   baby squid if you like
6 raw king prawns
¼ red pepper, diced
sea salt

Heat a little olive oil in a pan, add the onion and garlic with a pinch of salt, and sauté until the onion softens. Add the chorizo and sauté for 3–4 minutes, until it begins to crisp around the edges.

Add the turmeric, paprika and rice and stir well. Pour in half the stock and simmer until almost absorbed, stirring regularly. Add nearly all the remaining stock and simmer until the mixture is drying out a little. Test the rice to check texture: if almost cooked, add the seafood and pepper, but if still a little firm, add some more vegetable stock and continue cooking. Once the seafood and pepper have been added, cook for 5–8 minutes to cook through, stirring often to prevent sticking.

## Chicken, bacon and vegetable tray bake

**Chicken, bacon and vegetable tray bake** I have to admit that some days I just want to spend as little time in the kitchen as possible. Throwing together an all-in-one tray bake is often the way to go, and this is a perfect example. Really, you can put together any combination you want.

**SERVES 1–2**

1 courgette, sliced
    into rounds
1 red pepper, halved,
    seeded and sliced
½ red onion, cut into
    thin wedges
2–3 chicken legs
100g bacon lardons
3–4 sun-dried tomatoes,
    each chopped into 3
1 tablespoon pitted
    kalamata olives
2 bay leaves
sea salt and cracked
    black pepper

Preheat the oven to 200°C/400°F/Gas mark 6.

Place the courgette, pepper and onion in a roasting tin. Place the chicken legs on top and sprinkle over the lardons, sun-dried tomatoes and olives. Season with salt and cracked black pepper and throw in the bay leaves.

Bake in the oven for about 10 minutes, then remove from the oven and stir everything around to ensure that the rendered fat from the chicken and bacon coats the vegetables evenly.

Return to the oven for another 25 minutes, stirring again if you want to avoid sticking (I quite like the caramelised flavour you get on peppers and onions when they stick a little).

# Side dishes

*These side dishes represent another opportunity to up the nutrient density and create a meal that adheres to all three of the important principles outlined in this book.*

## Balsamic roasted roots

Balsamic roasted roots I always play around with ways of cooking root vegetables, using a variation of syrups and spices, and one of my new favourites is a balsamic roast. The sharpness of the vinegar really sits nicely with the sweetness of the roots.

**SERVES 2–4**

1 parsnip, scrubbed clean and cut into thick batons
1 large beetroot, scrubbed clean and cut into wedges
1 small sweet potato, scrubbed clean and cut into wedges
1 red onion, cut into wedges
1 tablespoon olive oil
3 tablespoons balsamic vinegar

Preheat the oven to 200°C/400°F/Gas mark 6.

Place all the vegetables in a roasting tin. Drizzle the olive oil and 1 tablespoon of the balsamic vinegar over them, and toss well.

Roast in the oven for about 15 minutes, then remove from the oven and drizzle over a second tablespoon of balsamic vinegar. Return to the oven for another 10 minutes. Remove again from the oven, add the remaining balsamic vinegar, toss well and roast for a final 15 minutes.

# Butter beans with bacon, rosemary and pumpkin seeds

This super simple side has a wonderful indulgent flavour, and is a real energy dish, with good fats, complex carbs and B vitamins all creating a filling slow burner.

**SERVES 2**

100g bacon lardons
1 x 400g tin butter
   beans, drained
½ clove garlic, finely chopped
1 tablespoon pumpkin seeds
1 teaspoon fresh rosemary
   leaves, finely chopped

Cook the lardons in a small pan over a high heat for 1–2 minutes, until they start to release their fat.

Throw in the remaining ingredients and cook for another 10 minutes, stirring often, but allowing the lardons to get a little crisper around the edges.

# Rainbow rice

Rainbow rice This is not only a fun way of making rice a little less dull, but it also notches up the nutrient value of your meal.

**SERVES 2**
120g brown rice
olive oil, for cooking
½ carrot, finely diced
½ red pepper, finely diced
½ large red onion, finely diced
½ courgette, finely diced
1 handful baby spinach,
   shredded

Place the brown rice in a saucepan and cover with boiling water. Simmer for around 20 minutes until soft, then drain thoroughly.

Meanwhile, heat a little olive oil in a pan, add the carrot, pepper, onion and courgette, and sauté for 8–10 minutes, until all of the vegetables are soft. Add the spinach and sauté for another minute or two until the spinach has wilted.

Add the drained rice to the vegetables and mix well to combine evenly.

**Chana saag** I'm pretty besotted with curry and have at least one a week. This lovely side contains two of my staple curry companions – spinach and chickpeas. Simple and sumptuous.

**SERVES 2**

olive oil, for cooking
2 cloves garlic, finely chopped
4 large tomatoes, diced
1 x 400g tin chickpeas, drained
¼ teaspoon ground cumin
½ teaspoon ground turmeric
½ teaspoon ground cinnamon
2 handfuls baby spinach

Heat a little olive oil in a pan, add the garlic, and sauté for 2 minutes. Add the tomatoes, chickpeas and spices and simmer for about 10 minutes more, until the juice from the tomatoes reduces a little.

Add the spinach and simmer until the spinach has wilted.

## White bean mustard mash

I absolutely love mustard mash. The problem is, regular spuds can be a bit of a starch bomb and have a very high glycaemic impact, which is why I save them just for my Sunday lunch. Using white beans gives you a gorgeous, creamy mash and a much more slow-burn option, with a whole lot of nutrients too, such as copious amounts of brilliant B vitamins.

**SERVES 2**

1 x 400g tin cannellini
   beans, drained
2 tablespoons olive oil
1 teaspoon English mustard
sea salt and black pepper

Put the beans in a pan and heat up gently. Mash them using a potato masher. Add the olive oil and mash again until it reaches a creamy consistency. Stir in the mustard and season to taste.

# Green beans and fennel with anchovy and capers

This simple side is a taste explosion, and ticks all the right boxes in terms of nutrition. A great side dish for fish and white meat, as well as Mediterranean-style dishes.

**SERVES 2**

140g green beans, trimmed
olive oil, for cooking
1 fennel bulb, sliced
2 teaspoons capers
30g anchovy fillets
   in oil, chopped

Blanch the green beans in boiling water for 2 minutes, then drain and set aside to dry a little.

Heat a little olive oil in a pan, add the fennel and green beans, and sauté for about 10 minutes, until the fennel has softened. Add the capers and gently stir in the anchovies.

## Citrus roasted roots

Citrus and root vegetables may sound a bit odd, but I tried it one Christmas and absolutely loved it! Give it a bash and you'll see what a joy it is.

**SERVES 2**

1 small sweet potato, diced
½ swede, diced
2–3 parsnips, cut into
   long wedges
grated zest of 1 orange
   and juice of ½
1 tablespoon olive oil
sea salt and cracked
   black pepper

Preheat the oven to 200°C/400°F/Gas mark 6.

Place the vegetables in a roasting tin. Add the orange juice and olive oil with salt and pepper to taste, and toss well.

Roast in the oven for 25–30 minutes, until the vegetables are soft and starting to turn golden. Add the orange zest and mix well before serving.

# Spiced wine-braised red cabbage

I absolutely adore this with a Sunday roast. It's redolent of winter, but I can happily devour it all year round!

**SERVES 2**
olive oil, for cooking
½ small red cabbage,
  finely shredded
3 teaspoons goji berries
½ clove garlic,
  finely chopped
1 small red chilli,
  finely chopped
3 tablespoons red wine
½ teaspoon ground
  cinnamon

Heat a little olive oil in a pan, add the cabbage, goji berries, garlic and chilli, and sauté for about 5 minutes, stirring frequently.

Add the red wine and simmer until the wine has reduced right down. Add the cinnamon and cook for another minute before serving.

# Garlic and chilli broccoli This is a great little side dish. Whilst it has a real Asian flavour, it lends itself to many types of cuisine and is great with chicken or fish.

**SERVES 2**

1 head of broccoli
olive oil, for cooking
2 large cloves garlic,
  finely sliced
1 red chilli, finely sliced
1 teaspoon runny honey
2 teaspoons untoasted
  sesame oil
3 teaspoons soy sauce

Break the broccoli into florets and place in a pan. Cover with boiling water and simmer for about 5 minutes or until they have turned a brighter green and are soft enough to push a fork into with only a little pressure. Drain, then allow to dry out.

Heat a little olive oil in a pan, add the garlic, and sauté for about 1 minute. Add the chilli and drained broccoli and stir-fry for a minute or so.

Add the honey, sesame oil and soy sauce and cook for 2 minutes, stirring, until the honey begins to caramelise and the sauce is dark and sticky.

# Griddled courgettes with mint, dill and feta

This is an amazing side dish that brings back memories of holidays in Greece and Cyprus. It works well as a BBQ side or with any cooked fish and seafood.

**SERVES 2**

1 large courgette
olive oil, for cooking
small sprig fresh
   mint, chopped
small sprig fresh
   dill, chopped
80g feta cheese
cracked black pepper

Cut the courgette lengthways into long slices about 5mm thick.

Drizzle a little olive oil into a ridged griddle pan and place over a high heat until almost smoking. Lay the courgette slices in the hot pan and cook on each side until dark char lines appear and the slices are soft. Remove from the heat and allow to cool a little.

Place the griddled courgette in a bowl with the mint and dill. Crumble in the feta, add a little cracked black pepper and toss well.

# Desserts

*Now, desserts aren't particularly my strongest point, but I am partial to a sweet treat once in a while. I know there aren't many here, but what is here is tasty and ticks at the very least one of the boxes each time.*

# Chocolate 'ice cream' This is a fantastic ice cream alternative – simple to make and satisfying too. You can make it as it is for a softer texture, or freeze it for slightly longer for something firmer.

**SERVES 2–3**

1½ bananas, peeled,
  chopped and frozen
3 tablespoons cocoa powder
2 tablespoons coconut milk
½ teaspoon vanilla extract

Place all the ingredients in a powerful blender or food processor and blitz to a soft ice cream texture. If you want it firmer, transfer to a tub with a lid and place in the freezer. After 30 minutes, give it a stir, and if you want it firmer still, put it back in the freezer for another 30 minutes, stir and carry on in this way until it is your preferred consistency.

## Flax banana bread

This has a lovely cakey vibe and is great with the Chocolate 'Ice Cream' on page 169, a little crème fraîche, or on its own.

**MAKES 1 LOAF**

2 very ripe bananas
(skins turning brown),
peeled
175ml milk
85g runny honey
200g wholemeal flour
2 tablespoons ground
flaxseeds
1 tablespoon baking powder
1½ teaspoons ground
cinnamon

Preheat the oven to 180°C/350°F/Gas mark 4 and line a small loaf tin with baking parchment.

Mash the bananas in a bowl. Add the milk and honey and whisk together. Add the flour, ground flaxseeds, baking powder and cinnamon, and mix well until evenly combined.

Transfer the mixture to the lined tin and bake in the oven for 45–55 minutes, until golden brown, and when you slide a knife into the centre, it comes out clean.

# Baked fruit with spiced yoghurt and flax sprinkle Simple, wholesome and comforting.

**SERVES 2**

1 apple, cored and cut
   into wedges
1 pear, cored and cut
   into wedges
olive oil, for drizzling
4 tablespoons natural yoghurt
1 teaspoon vanilla extract
½ teaspoon ground cinnamon
½ teaspoon ground ginger
generous pinch black pepper
1 tablespoon ground flaxseeds
1 teaspoon brown sugar

Preheat the oven to 180°C/350°F/Gas mark 4.

Place the fruit wedges in a baking tray. Drizzle with a tiny amount of olive oil and bake in the oven for 20–30 minutes, until soft, squidgy and caramelising nicely.

Combine the yoghurt, vanilla and spices in a bowl and stir well. Mix the ground flaxseeds and brown sugar together in a separate bowl.

Divide the baked fruit between 2 bowls. Add some spiced yoghurt to each and top with the flax sprinkle.

## Char-grilled peaches with 'toffee' sauce

Ok, so this dish can't be called low GI, but it is a lovely dessert free of nasty trans fats that can scupper fatty acid balance, and gives quite a nice range of nutrients, such as carotenoids and a few minerals. It's a treat...but not too bad!

**SERVES 2**

2 peaches, stones removed
   and flesh cut into wedges
20g pitted dates,
   finely chopped
10g butter

Preheat a griddle pan until hot. Place the peach wedges in the pan and cook until dark char marks appear on the flesh. Turn them over and repeat on the other side.

For the sauce, combine the dates and 4 tablespoons water in a pan and place over a high heat. Simmer until the dates start to break down into a paste, then add the butter and stir until it has melted into the mixture to create a sauce.

Place the peach wedges in 2 bowls and spoon the gooey sauce over the top.

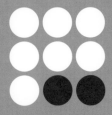

# Snacks

*Snacking can sometimes be people's downfall. Having a few healthier snack items prepared and ready is a perfect way to prevent this.*

## Chocolate peanut butter cups

I'm not sure there is a better combination than chocolate and peanut butter! These taste off-the-charts amazing, and they are actually pretty good for you too! Flavonoids, minerals, B vitamins, and much lower GI than their shop-bought incarnations.

**MAKES 12–15**

325g high-quality dark chocolate (at least 80% cocoa solids)
260g natural peanut butter (with no added sugar or oil)

Bring some water to the boil in a saucepan and, as soon as it boils, remove from the heat and place a glass heatproof bowl on top, making sure the base of the bowl isn't touching the water. Add half the chocolate and stir constantly as it slowly melts.

Half-fill 12–15 mini paper cupcake cases or trimmed down regular cases with the melted chocolate, then place the cases in the fridge to cool and set.

Once set, remove from the fridge and add a dollop of peanut butter on top of the set chocolate, leaving space around the edges.

Melt the remaining chocolate in the same way, then pour over the peanut butter, to completely fill the cases. Return to the fridge until set.

# Tuna cucumber cups This is a great little snack or canapé.

**MAKES 10–12**
1 x 112g tin tuna, drained
1 tablespoon mayonnaise
juice of ½ lemon
¼ teaspoon ground cumin
½ red chilli, finely chopped
1 large cucumber
sea salt and black pepper

Place the tuna, mayonnaise, lemon juice, cumin and chilli together in a bowl, with salt and pepper to taste. Mix well to combine.

Cut the cucumber into sections about 2.5cm long. Scoop out most of the seedy centres, leaving about 5mm at the base, to make cups.

Fill the cucumber cups with the tuna mixture.

## Sardine spread This delicious spread is a real omega-3 hit and lends itself very well to vegetable crudités, as well as making a great sandwich filler.

**SERVES 1–2**
1 x 84g tin sardines
   in olive oil
3 tablespoons natural
   yoghurt
juice of ½ lemon
small bunch fresh parsley
small bunch fresh dill
sea salt and black pepper

Spoon the sardines and their oil into a food processor. Add the remaining ingredients, with salt and pepper to taste, and process to a smooth spread.

# Broad bean and feta dip

This is seriously addictive stuff. Fresh, flavoursome, creamy – you can't ask for much more really! Great with toasted pitta, corn chips, oat cakes and vegetable crudités.

**SERVES 2–3**

1 x 400g tin broad
  beans, drained
100g feta cheese
juice of ½ lime
1 tablespoon flaxseed oil
sea salt and black pepper

Place all the ingredients in a food processor (reserving a few broad beans for texture), with salt and pepper to taste, and process to a smooth dip. Stir in the reserved broad beans and serve.

**Artichoke houmous** I love making artichoke-based dips and this is one of my favourites so far. Artichoke is a powerhouse ingredient with benefits for the liver and digestive health.

**SERVES 2–3**
1 x 400g tin chickpeas,
    drained
1 x 100g tin artichoke
    hearts in oil, drained
1 clove garlic, peeled
    and roughly chopped
1 tablespoon flaxseed oil
    (or olive oil)
sea salt

Place all the ingredients in a blender or food processor, with salt to taste, and blend to a thick houmous.

Serve with vegetable crudités and oat cakes. It also tastes great dolloped on top of a baked sweet potato.

# Slow roasted squash and walnut dip

You can use any squash you like here, but my personal recommendation, if you can find it, is the crown prince variety. Butternut or festival are great too, as is the humble pumpkin. They are all packed with carotenoids and offer a very slow-burning energy source.

**SERVES 2–3**

1 small squash, peeled, seeded and diced
2 cloves garlic, unpeeled
olive oil, for cooking
200g walnuts
3 tablespoons flaxseed oil
sea salt and black pepper

Preheat the oven to 200°C/400°F/Gas mark 6.

Place the diced squash in a roasting tin. Flatten the garlic using the flat side of a large knife, remove the papery skins, then break up the cloves amongst the squash. Add a drizzle of olive oil and a good pinch of salt and pepper, then roast in the oven for about 35 minutes, or until the squash is very soft and beginning to caramelise at the edges, and the garlic is caramelised and gooey.

Transfer to a food processor, add the walnuts and flaxseed oil and blitz to a smooth dip.

# Anchovy and sun-dried tomato spread

This has a serious umami hit! I love this spread on toasted soda bread, or smeared all over an oat cake. Gorgeous stuff!

**SERVES 1–2**

1 x 140g jar sun-dried
   tomatoes in oil, drained
30g tin anchovies,
   with their oil
½ clove garlic, finely chopped
½ red chilli, finely chopped
pinch smoked paprika
   (optional)

Place all the ingredients in a food processor and process to a smooth spread.

# INDEX

Want to work in food, health, and wellness?
Want to study without rigid time commitments
and without breaking the bank?

**Consider studying at Dale Pinnock's**
## THE SCHOOL OF CULINARY MEDICINE

- Evidence based, applied, and practical.
- Study anywhere, anytime. Fit the course around your life.
- No tight deadlines or timescales, take as long as you want.
- Encourages *your* creativity and teaches you how to build recipes around the science with confidence.
- Developed by one of the country's leading voices in nutrition and health.

Accredited and CPD registered.
Our 'Diploma in Culinary Medicine' has been accredited by the CMA and the FNTP, and has been awarded a value of 5 CPD points to qualified NTs by the FNTP

www.schoolofculinarymedicine.com
enquiries@schoolofculinarymedicine.com
03450 523 595

## RESOURCES

### DIABETES UK
Diabetes UK is the most widely known diabetes organisation in the UK. Their website is a great resource for information on diabetes and its management.
**diabetes.org.uk**

### BRITISH HEART FOUNDATION
This is probably the best known organisation championing heart health. Their website is a great resource for everything from statistics and medical breakthrough information, through to practical everyday tips for looking after your heart.
**bhf.org.uk**

### BRITISH DIETETIC ASSOCIATION
The BDA have developed a great deal of factsheets that are available for free. These factsheets comprise information about specific illnesses/disorders/system health. They also offer advice on dietary changes etc.
**bda.uk.com/foodfacts/hypertension**

### LOVE OMEGA
Love Omega is a website that offers a broad spectrum of information on omega-3 fatty acids and their role in health, how to eat more of them, and interesting articles too. It also has an omega predictor tool – an online questionnaire that will give you guidance as to how your omega-3/-6 ratios maybe doing.
**loveomega.com**

## Acknowledgements

Clare Hulton – we continue to go from strength to strength.
Zoie Wainwright – manager extraordinaire and all-round incredible headcase.
Tanya Murkett – as always you bring the joy and the sunshine.
All the team at Quadrille; Smith & Gilmour; Martin Poole; Aya Nishimura;
Catherine Tyldesley; Gaby Roslin; Mum & Dad; Ramsay & Candy; and all
the wonderful people that are consistently supporting me.

Publishing director: Sarah Lavelle
Creative director: Helen Lewis
Senior editor: Céline Hughes
Art direction and design: Smith & Gilmour
Photography: Martin Poole
Food stylist: Aya Nishimura
Props stylist: Polly Webb-Wilson
Production: Tom Moore

First published in 2016 by Quadrille Publishing
Pentagon House, 52–54 Southwark Street, London SE1 1UN

Quadrille Publishing is an imprint of Hardie Grant
www.hardiegrant.com.au
www.quadrille.co.uk

Text © 2016 Dale Pinnock
Photography © 2016 Martin Poole
Design and layout © 2016 Quadrille Publishing

Cataloguing in Publication Data: a catalogue record for this book
is available from the British Library.

978 184949 559 2

Printed in China